Exotic Gardeni in Cool Climates

Myles Challis is an established garden designer and contractor, and was the first to specialize in exotic gardens. He has won awards for his gardens at the Chelsea Flower Show, and has been the subject of many magazine and newspaper articles.

His greatest source of inspiration was a book written at the turn of the century called *A Gloucestershire Wild Garden* in which Henry Cooke describes how he created the garden which ultimately became the setting for the film *The Assam Garden*.

Myles Challis was the instigator in the development of a movement, now known as the 'exoticists', a group of people including nurserymen and enthusiasts, whose aim is to encourage the interest in growing these beautiful plants.

MYLES CHALLIS

Exotic Gardening in Cool Climates

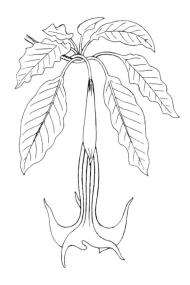

Datura cornigera

WITH TWENTY-FOUR COLOUR PLATES
BY MICHAEL NICHOLSON
AND NINETEEN LINE DRAWINGS
BY THE AUTHOR

FOURTH ESTATE · LONDON

First published in Great Britain in 1988 as *The Exotic Garden* by
Fourth Estate Limited
289 Westbourne Grove
London W11 2QA

This paperback edition, with a new introduction, first published 1994

A catalogue record for this book is available from the British Library.

ISBN 1–85702–187–8

Printed in Great Britain by Bath Press Limited

CONTENTS

CHAPTER FOUR 81

CHAPTER FIVE 99

APPENDICES 161

INDEX 169

LIST OF ILLUSTRATIONS

Colour Plates

Appearing between pages 34 and 35
Gunnera manicata
Musa ensete
Hedychium coccineum 'Tara'
Trachycarpus fortunei

Appearing between pages 66 and 67
Polygonum cuspidatum 'Spectabile'
Hibiscus moscheutos 'Southern Belle'
Tetrapanax papyriferus
Rheum tanguticum
Acanthus mollis latifolius
Arundo donax 'Variegata'
Canna generalis 'Wyoming' and *Melianthus major*
Embothrium coccineum

Appearing between pages 98 and 99
Datura cornigera
Canna iridiflora 'Ehemanni'
Ricinus gibsonii
Phyllostachys nigra
Hydrangea aspera
Canna 'Firebird'
Phormium tenax 'Purpureum'
Cardiocrinum giganteum

Appearing between pages 130 and 131
Dicksonia antarctica
The author's garden, London
Phyllostachys pubescens

Line Drawings

INTRODUCTION

Man has long sought paradise, be it often subconsciously, but fantasy can become reality and no more so than in the creation of an exotic garden. The most spectacular gardens in the world are those of the tropics, where the rich diversity of form and colour is unparalleled. However, one does not have to live in close proximity to the equator in order to create a garden of this type: the essence of a tropical garden is luxuriant greenery and splashes of vibrant colour. All this can be had, even in a cool climate – the lushness of leaf in palms, bananas and bamboos, and the dazzling colour in the blooms of hibiscus, daturas, gingers and cannas. It may come as a surprise to learn that there are hardy palms, bamboos and even bananas, and a vast range of other exotic-looking plants that are hardy or near hardy: cordylines, phormiums and gunneras, for example. From these it is easy to create wonderful tropical looking gardens.

Although the cool climate of such places as the British Isles may seem to impose limitations, a far wider range of plants can be grown than most people realise. It is in fact possible to create a garden the like of which might be found in the Mediterranean, the tropics or even a rain-forest – a strong contrast to the type of shrub and herbaceous planting usually encountered. If magic and mystery are usually the most sought-after qualities in a garden, these are certainly easily achievable in an exotic garden. This book will show you how to create your own paradise, using an exciting range of plants which most people will have never before encountered.

There is one more essential ingredient needed to complete the exotic effect: water. Any water feature, pond or stream is sufficient, preferably with a waterfall or cascade, so long as it is natural and informal. Exotic plants do not lend themselves to the hard, straight lines of formal beds and borders but require the unrestrained curves of winding paths or lawn edges. Most possess strong architectural qualities and are striking even when used individually, but when arranged or grouped together their great variety of form can produce stunning effects.

A few of the plants may be familiar. Bamboos, for example, are occasionally used in ordinary herbaceous or shrub borders, but they are infinitely more attractive when placed with other hardy exotics as they complement one another. Large leaves of any kind can give an air of tropical lushness, and so even plants such as hostas or ligularias can be used, and when mixed with more foreign-looking subjects they take on a totally new character.

For the adventurous, seeking something totally new, this exciting form of gardening cannot fail to please. It is not perhaps for those that are daunted by size, for with few exceptions most of these plants are not only strong and vigorous, but often attain quite large proportions in a relatively short period of time. As such it is a very 'instant' form of gardening. This does not mean however that the exotic gardener has to possess a very large garden. An average town garden of, say, 80′ × 20′ would be more than adequate to display a good selection of these beautiful plants.

The fast growth rate of many of them also means that planting costs can be cut by initially purchasing smaller specimens, which will become large and give the garden an established look in a comparatively short period of time. And since tropical plants require an informal setting all the most expensive elements of hard landscaping, such as brick walls, paving and pergolas, are eliminated. It is also a low-maintenance style of gardening: the plants require little or no pruning or preening and can be left to develop just as nature intended. Their main requirement is that they should be watered regularly in hot weather and perhaps fed occasionally. Many plants, especially those with big leaves, possess great weed-suppressing qualities – yet another advantage.

The only expenditure likely to be required, other than on the plants themselves, is on the water feature, essential in an exotic garden. Certain plants, such as bamboos and especially gunneras, are not only seen at their best by water but actually benefit from and indeed require additional moisture. The water feature should, where possible, be the main focal point and highlight of the garden.

Despite their exotic appearance eighty per cent of the plants recommended in this book are completely hardy, and while some of them may require shelter from strong winds, they generally require no more attention and are no more difficult to grow than any ordinary trees and shrubs. The remaining twenty per cent of plants dealt with in this book can easily be grown in a conservatory or greenhouse. These are plants which, though they have a strong constitution, will not bear frost, but if grown in containers as I suggest will ornament both the garden in summer and the conservatory in winter. They are the most spectacular plants that can be grown out of doors in the summer months in cool climates. What could be more exotic than the datura with its huge, pendulous, intoxicatingly scented, trumpet-shaped flowers? Yet it is the easiest of plants to grow, compared to the majority of indoor plants.

By late summer most gardens in cool climates are looking jaded and frazzled, but the hardy exotics are not only in the peak of condition but still making vigorous growth and will continue to do so until the first frosts. Exotics extend the summer season, a particular advantage in countries where the summers are relatively short. Tender exotics, wintered under glass can also extend the season in the spring by adding instant interest and beauty to the garden at a time when many ordinary plants are still developing. And many hardy exotics are evergreen, enabling the garden to be attractive all year round – a great asset in the winter months when many gardens look bleak.

So exotic gardening holds many advantages over more traditional prac-tices, particularly in terms of labour. Gardening is a pastime to be enjoyed and should not become a chore. It can have tremendous therapeutic powers, helping one to relax and unwind at the end of a stressful day, and the exotic garden especially, with its vigour and fruitfulness, seems to possess great comforting qualities, giving a tremendous sense of well-being. My garden has given me endless pleasure, gaining as it does in splendour year by year, a pleasure which has been shared by the many visitors who seem mesmerized by what is after all only 'what nature can produce'.

I was spellbound when taken to Kew Gardens for the first time at the age of seven. Stepping into one of the glasshouses I was engulfed by a forest of enormous leaves that seemed almost Brobdingnagian. Not many years after, having persuaded my father to install heating into a huge greenhouse that until then had stood empty in our garden, I began collecting a vast array of amazing equatorial plants, mostly with large leaves. Philodendrons and scindapsus climbed the walls and dead tree trunks, while under the shade of heliconias and palms, anthuriums, alocasias and calatheas with their strikingly patterned leaves flourished in the steamy heat. I had, through meeting nurserymen and plant hunters, built up a collection of the world's most spectacular tropical plants. I was also fortunate at the time in having a butterfly-collecting uncle, who on his many trips around the globe would occasionally send me a crate of assorted treasures from the plant kingdom which he had collected in some jungle here or there. But all good things must come to an end and the oil crisis brought a temporary end to my hobby; the collection had to be dispersed and sold off. The big-leaf bug, however, was still very much present in me, and after some research I began to discover, to my great delight I might add, that not all exotic-looking plants required the protection of the glasshouse. Big leaves do not come much larger than that of the gunnera, a hardy plant and one of my first discoveries. To this I added bamboos, phormiums, fatsias, lysichitums, petasites and even a hardy palm. My first exotic garden was distinctly 'foreign' in character but it was by no means 'exotic' enough for my satisfaction.

It was a few years later that I stumbled upon *A Gloucestershire Wild Garden*, a book which was to prove to be my greatest source of inspiration. It was written anonymously at the turn of the century by a man called Henry Cooke, modestly calling himself 'the curator'. Cooke had served as surgeon-general in the army in India for some years, and loved the gardens he had seen there so much that he was determined on his return to England to re-create one as far as he could. On my first enounter with this book it fell open at a black and white photograph of a glade in Cooke's garden at the centre of which, in a collection of assorted exotics, towered two great Abyssinian banana trees. It was then that I realized that I could create a more tropical garden than I had ever thought possible.

Cooke's ambitions went beyond what most of us can aspire to, and even Cooke himself confessed to never being fully satisfied. But in a more modest way we can create and enjoy what gave immeasurable pleasure both to him and his visitors. 'There are few who visit me who are not impressed with the beauty and interest which a wild garden affords as compared with the ordinary garden,' he wrote. It is for you to agree or disagree, but if your taste is for the exotic and unusual, then I feel sure that you will find endless pleasure and interest in this new and exciting form of gardening.

ACKNOWLEDGEMENTS

I should like to thank the following people for allowing plants in their gardens to be photographed for this book and for their trouble and kindness in so doing: Mr J.D. Bond, Saville Gardens; Major J.A. Hibbert, Trebah; Beth Chatto; Mr D. Jones, City Parks Department; the staff of the Temperate Section, Kew; Tony Schilling, Wakehurst; and Anthony Rogers, Carwinion. Thanks also to Gay Gottlieb, Peter Partridge and Liz and John Bonython for their hospitality.

Finally, I owe a special debt of gratitude to Michael Nicholson, both for his expertise and for his inexhaustible patience and generosity, without which the photographic requirements of this book could not have been fulfilled.

MYLES CHALLIS

CHAPTER ONE

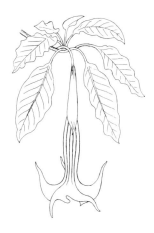

What Is Exotic Gardening and
What Are Its Merits?

•

A ll forms of gardening have their own particular merits, and it is no good being too dictatorial about which is the best for any particular garden or gardener. But the exotic garden is quite a radical departure from the more traditional styles of garden encountered in this country, so it is worth exploring its particular attractions and advantages.

The word 'exotic' is used here in a descriptive rather than technical sense – that is to say, the plants recommended are exotic in appearance, but not necessarily in origin. They are, in fact, remarkably easy plants to grow and maintain in our climate and, while they may remind us of some far-off tropical haven complete with parakeets and chattering monkeys, they do not require a hot or steamy climate to thrive. This is, of course, because most of them do not originate in tropical climes but in places such as New Zealand, China and Japan. Plants from these countries can be used to create splendidly exotic effects without an exotic climate.

The Victorians were the first to practise this form of gardening, and they probably contributed to the idea that it is a delicate and tricky occupation best left to expert botanists by referring to it as 'subtropical' gardening. In fact, subtropical gardening in the true sense of the word can be seen and practised only in such places as Florida. The nearest we have to it in the British Isles are the gardens of Tresco on the Isles of Scilly, which on the whole are of the drier, Mediterranean type, whereas in this book I shall be dealing with the more lush-leaved, moisture-loving plants. The Victorians' use of the term 'subtropical' is also misleading when one considers that the majority of the plants used (about 75 per cent) were hardy. The same is true of the plants I have included in this book. The bulk of them I shall refer to as 'hardy exotics'. These are frost-hardy, usually withstanding temperatures down to 14°F or lower if of European origin. But I have also included some 'tender exotics', plants which require the protection of a heated environment – house, conservatory or greenhouse – in winter. These plants usually prefer to be overwintered at about 45–50°F, and would either be killed or at least levelled to the ground by frost, though they might make new growth the following year. Any plant which will withstand a few degrees of frost for a limited period I have described as half-hardy or semi-hardy. And I have also included some more familiar plants – usually lower growing and flowering – if they particularly complement the exotics.

Plants with large, handsome and distinctive foliage give a garden a very luxuriant feel, especially when used in abundance and variety, and it is this effect of a lush profusion of striking shapes, sizes, textures and colours which the exotic garden aims to achieve. A garden is a place to relax in and such an effect is above all peaceful and restful. This must be partly because exotic foliage inevitably reminds us of warm places, where the pace of life is slow and languorous and the world of towns and roads, of offices and factories, is far away. And what could be more relaxing than a garden that is reminiscent of a place where we might take a summer holiday?

A further element in the restful qualities of the exotic garden is its reliance on the natural beauty of the plants themselves. Garden design has for too long emphasized formal and architectural alignments with scant regard for the plants themselves. A garden of terraces, patios and pergolas, of clipped rose bushes and formal beds full of annual plants arranged in serried ranks of colour, may be entirely in keeping with the style of a stately home or mansion, but most of us do not live in such places, nor do we have the time or money to maintain a formal garden all through the year. Even if we did, we might be forgiven for deciding that the note of constraint which is a key element in formal gardens is not one which we would wish to emphasize in our own gardens. In the exotic garden it is the architecture of the plants themselves that dictates the style, so that it can never be rigid or monotonous or dominated by straight lines and bands of colour. Each of the plants that I recommend in this book is a feature in itself, and its natural elegance and grace can only be diminished if attempts are made to define it within too formal a design. Far better to set off a plant with other contrasting plants than with paving, brickwork or other design elements with which it could never be naturally associated. An arrangement of exotics such as I shall describe later in this book will always be easier on the eye than an annual bed, where large blocks of colour are used with no respect for the individual beauty and character of the plants. The effect of freedom from constraint which the exotic garden achieves is surely desirable in any garden that is a place to enjoy and relax in rather than a formal showpiece designed to attract visitors on weekend afternoons.

Of course the exotic garden is a contrivance like any other. And, regardless of the style or form it takes, every garden has its own individuality, which should (and generally does) reflect that of its owner. The garden of a fastidious housewife may well be one of trim lawns and neat shrubberies, while that of an unconventional art teacher might be relatively untamed and wild, allowed to do its own thing. All styles of gardening, if tastefully carried out, are commendable. But two things are worth bearing in mind, First, there is no need to feel that the type of garden you grow is dictated by your environment. Just because you live in a cottage, that doesn't mean you should necessarily have a cottage-style garden; likewise, a walled city garden does not have to be dominated by paving and brickwork. Second, any style of gardening which is informal and free of constraint is far better able to accommodate the tastes and inclinations of the individual – and therefore more likely to satisfy the gardener – than any which is patrolled by straight edges and defined by anything other than the plants themselves.

Once we appreciate that plants have their own design and character and are not simply there to throw out colour in the form of flowers at certain times of year, then choosing plants for the garden becomes infinitely more exciting and rewarding. Of course flowering is a vital part of the life cycle of plants, as is the production of new growth and seeds. But by choosing plants for their flowers alone we restrict ourselves greatly, missing much, and risk having a very bleak garden in winter. In the exotic garden it is the foliage that provides the interest and beauty, with flowers an added bonus at certain times of year. This means that the exotic garden is attractive and lovely for many more months of the year than the average British garden – especially since many of the exotics are at their peak in late summer, by which time the traditional garden is beginning to look jaded and straggly. The tender exotics, in particular, are still making vigorous development at this time.

The bananas (*Musa*) and the tree ferns (*Dicksonia*) are pushing forth their largest leaves, the gingers (*Hedychium*) and the cannas are producing their grand flowers, along with the datura, which is still producing an abundance of huge, pendulous, white and fragrant blooms, having done so since the spring in a good year, and will continue to do so at least until October. When tender exotics are cultivated the season is also extended at the beginning of the summer, because plants overwintered indoors can be put outside in May, instantly adding interest to the garden at a time when many of the hardy plants are still in the early stages of development.

It is thus the permanence of foliage, as well as its innate architectural form and quality, that makes it of such value and importance in the exotic garden. 'The flower soon fades and is gone but the leaf carries on' is an adage which any gardener would be wise to bear in mind. And it should not take long to appreciate that the variety of foliage available is just as great as the variety of flowers we can grow. Its colours are generally more subtle – from rich purples to pale silvers, from vibrant greens to airy goldens – but there are also plenty of plants which boast brilliant oranges and pinks, and it should not be forgotten that foliage often changes colour quite dramatically during the course of a season. The contrasts available when plants are chosen primarily for their foliage are infinitely delightful, especially in the exotic garden which displays so many plants with huge and bold leaves, the perfect companion to those with smaller or more delicately cut foliage. Such a contrast is also of value because the finer leaves are best appreciated close to, while large leaves are still handsome and distinctive from afar.

Our summers are relatively short in these isles – the spring can be late, cold and wet, the autumn sudden and unexpected. But it is important that our gardens can still give pleasure during the average of seven months of the year when we are unable to sit out in them. In addition to those plants which lose their leaves at the end of the season, the exotic garden is also rich in evergreens, which add so much to the winter picture. Large subjects like the Chusan palm (*Trachycarpus fortunei*), the many bamboos and the eucalyptus dominate, while at the lower level the almost always pristine *Fatsia japonica*, the loquat (*Eriobotrya japonica*) and the lovely *Rhododendron macabeanum* help to fill in, along with the New Zealand flax (*Phormium tenax*). These and many others can be enjoyed all year round, if only from the warmth of a room with a view over the garden.

If we are also cultivating the tender exotics then we have these to enjoy in the house or conservatory during the winter months. Nearly all the tender exotics remain in superb condition through the cold months, continuing to grow and, in the case of the datura, perhaps even gracing us with a few magnificent blooms.

Foliage has come to be more and more appreciated in recent years, especially plants like the hosta – there are now hosta societies both in this country and in the USA. It is too early to say whether this implies a general improvement in taste, but I would like to think so. I am, however, very much convinced that gardening trends are not influenced solely by the individual, but also by the level of information available, and the gardening world still concentrates almost exclusively on the cultivation of flowers. As William Robinson pointed out, 'How is a man to make gardens wisely if he does not know what has to be grown in them?'

I hope this book will provide information on a range of plants that may not be familiar to the average gardener, as well as pointing out new ways of using more familiar plants (though often the less well known varieties) in the setting of the exotic garden to which they are so well suited. It may be worth emphasizing again that the hardy and tender exotics introduced in this book are not 'difficult' plants. They do not require specialist knowledge, or extensive experience, or that mysterious and unlikely asset, 'green fingers'. In fact, by virtue of their adaptability to different conditions, the exotics are often robust, free-growing plants which are more likely to grow excessively than dwindle away at the first sign of adverse weather. And in terms of maintenance they require far less pruning and preening than many more traditional plants; I estimate that a small garden of exotics would require rather less expenditure in terms of time and money to keep in good condition than a single bed of annuals.

The exotic garden has many virtues, then, and no particular vices. Its season is long, its maintenance low, its interest abundant and its restful qualities unparalleled. It concentrates on plants which have something to offer at all seasons of the year, and it makes full use of the innate beauty and grace of the design nature has bestowed on them. Above all, it is a relaxing

place, both subtle and dramatic, varied and harmonious, a place which ideally should remind us of warmer, more restful climes. Compare all this with what the more traditional garden has to offer and surely the scales cannot help but tip in favour of the exotic garden. I hope that these and the following pages will bring many of you to appreciate the benefits which this style of garden bestows and inspire you to try it for yourselves. It is as yet a very little practised or explored form of gardening, but one that surely deserves wider appreciation.

Exotic Gardening
in Other Countries

•

Most gardening books for obvious and practical reasons are devoted to the culture of plants suited to the climate of a ·particular country of latitude. Here we are not bound by those restrictions, as the form of gardening advocated in this book can be adopted for many other countries and regions, especially the warmer ones. The south of France, Italy, Spain, Portugal, the Dordogne – much of southern Europe, in fact – are all ideal places climatically speaking for the creation of a garden of this type, if irrigation is supplied in areas of low rainfall. People living in these countries who wish to have beautiful gardens are accustomed to providing extensive irrigation, unless they are content with having a drier Mediterranean garden. With the warmer climate and sufficient moisture many of the plants, especially the tender exotics, would flourish and luxuriate even more than they would here in Britain, and in some cases many of them would not have to be wintered under glass, or perhaps only for a short period. Another advantage of such places as the

(Opposite) *Lilium canadense*

south of France and Italy is that many of the plants required for exotic gardening, such as palms and bamboos, are available locally, and are therefore less expensive than in Britain, where they have to be imported.

Many people now have second homes in these countries and could easily set up a garden of this type. It is wise to start by investigating the local winter weather conditions, obtaining average minimum temperatures, so as not to risk losing any plants. Some idea of what can be grown can be ascertained simply by observing what is growing in neighbouring gardens. For example, if a datura is growing quite happily outside, then the area is very likely to be frost-free and you could safely plant any of the tender exotics. Do not forget that in many warmer countries, especially in coastal areas, winter gales are often common, and in these circumstances shelter, preferably in the form of trees and hedging, should be established before serious planting is undertaken. And if you will be living there for only part of the year, you must consider whether plants will survive in your absence if there is no one to look after them. In warm places watering will be the main consideration.

But in general the cultivation of these plants in southern Europe is easy and will be extremely successful. Naturally exotic-looking plants will also often associate well with the native vegetation.

Henry Cooke's Description of His Exotic Garden

P erhaps my estimation of the merits of the exotic garden should be complemented by a more lyrical description of its special charms. There can surely have been no more ambitious and enthusiastic proponent of the exotic garden than Henry Cooke, whose book *A Gloucestershire Wild Garden*, written at the turn of the century, was such an inspiration to me. He refers to his garden as 'wild' or 'subtropical', but its principles are much the same as I advocate in this book. Here is his chapter entitled 'The Special Claims of the Wild Garden':

There are few who visit me who are not impressed with the beauty and interest which a wild garden affords as compared with the ordinary garden, with its laid out beds of annuals or perennials. There is certainly a charm in picturesque effect and freedom from all constraint which such a system insures.

The presence of stately trees, the charm of water, and the luxuriance of large foliaged plants, united with the colouring of the flowers, yield a picture which appeals to every eye, while the contrast of colours afforded by the dissimilar tints of the Coniferae and shrubs, which find a fit place amidst the flowering plants and the broken outlines given by the varying heights of the shrubs and trees, relieves the general effect from all feeling of sameness and tameness which, by comparison, the ordinary garden is not free from.

It is for this reason that I have advocated the use of plants with striking foliage and great dissimilarity of form, which alone combine to produce broad results, and the very nature of the wild garden renders the intermixture of shrubs with flowers a natural consequence – nay, an essential demand. Amidst the beds, whether small or large, of the ordinary garden this is inconvenient, and with laid-out beds of any sort the use of plants of unusual size is contra-indicated and embarrassing, yet large foliaged plants, raising their graceful or massive foliage far above the ordinary level, give an effect of freedom and luxuriance which nothing else can rival.

The various species of Conifers afford materials for use in contrast of colour and of form, and their mere formality of outline is no drawback, but rather the contrary, for it lends to contrast, and accentuates the charm of the spreading freedom of other more graceful forms of foliage. The dark green of the Retinosporas, with their compact habit, yield a pleasant contrast to the tints of the golden Thujas. The wide-spreading, almost naked limbs of the

Auraucaria contrast most efficiently with the massive forms of the dark green Yew, the softer texture and rich bronzy red of the Cryptomeria with the geometric regularity and brighter tints of the Silver Pine, the towering height of the Wellingtonia with the more diminutive form of the Cypress, and the extending branches of the *Pinus excelsa* with the compact foliage of the Arctic Thujopsis.

Then, again, the various species of Maples (which I have mentioned elsewhere) yield the strongest contrasts of colour – green and white, pure white, rich red, and dark purple – and judiciously placed are themselves sources of colour with the broadest effects, which mere flowering plants can hardly supply.

As regards variety of form, the many families of plants which I have described and advocated yield the widest contrasts, accentuating the peculiar beauty of outline possessed by each other. The enormous yet most symmetrically outlined leaves of the Gunnera render more sylph-like the slender, gracefully arching foliage of the Eulalia in its proximity. The shield-shaped leaves of the Peltandra or of the great Saxifrage increase the effect of the spear-like stems and long, narrow leaves of the Bulrush on the long bank of the pond, and the high, gracefully swaying fronds of the Bamboos accentuate the charm of the placid, oval-outlined leaves of the Water-lilies at their feet, while above all may tower the great leaves of the Abyssinian Musa, different alike in form and hue.

These are but a fraction of the effects to be obtained in the untrammelled constitution of the wild garden, and no other will easily admit of such an arrangement.

And this is aided and increased by the natural essentials of the site, its absence of formality, its natural freedom from restraint, the broken and uneven formation of the ground, the diversity afforded in the sky-reflected and tree-mirrored surface of the water, the free-growing, unmown stretches of grass, with the background of forest-trees encircling and forming the framework of the picture.

There is interest here which never flags, no presence of a monotony which tires, no necessity for the constant use of the lawn-mower to insure the requisite neatness which a formal garden demands, or the planting-out of beds of annuals. Summer and spring, autumn and even winter, produce their own special interests, though, indeed, the rich, hot summer – even the almost subtropical summer of the past year – enriches its glories and enhances its effects of colour and form, and presents the garden in its greatest beauty. And while under such conditions the laid-out garden flags and droops from want of moisture, the wild garden and its denizens grow and luxuriate under the hot sun.

It has been a contrast and a relief this past summer to leave the sun-dried Rosary or the heat-smitten parterre and wander amidst the deep shade or light-enhanced colour in the wild garden, and to watch the rapid growth of luxuriance which the unusual temperature has caused in the sun-loving exotics, the richly flowering and luxuriant leaved Cannas, the rapid-growing, towering shoots of the Bamboos, or the truly grand leaves of the Banana, ever increasing in height and width in the still, hot atmosphere of the season. Would that we could always have such seasons! They would never dry up our hopes or dissipate our expectations in the subtropical wild garden as they may in the flower-garden proper, but give a fuller development and a richer consummation of all that we desire in this most charming of Nature's gifts, the subtropical wild garden.

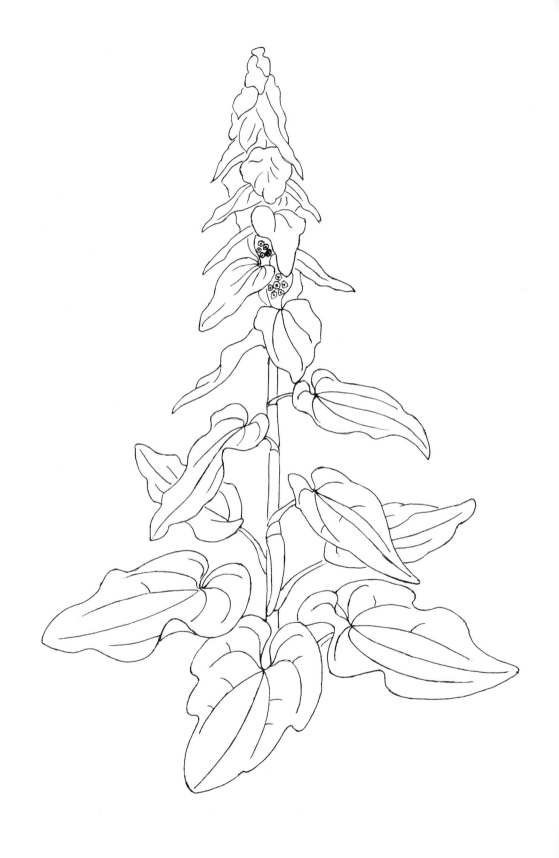

The Aim of This Book

•

I have tried with this book to encourage an interest in exotic gardening amongst all kinds of people, whether they have a small back garden in the city or a large country garden to experiment with. Such is its adaptability to different circumstances and the pleasure it has to offer that I am inclined to feel confident that more and more people will adopt this style of gardening – and that a general improvement in the knowledgeability and good temper of the population at large will be the result! However, it is upon my readers that the success of this book and its subject ultimately depends. As far as critics are concerned, I would only echo again the words of my predecessor, Henry Cooke:

> One does not write for critics, and I can only hope that, should any such one read this book, he may be a good one in the best sense of the word.

One is bound in any bold venture to step on a few toes, but such is progress.

(Opposite) *Rheum alexandrae*

CHAPTER TWO

The Early Plant Collectors
and Their Introductions and the
Invention of Exotic or 'Subtropical'
Gardening

•

U ntil the arrival of the great landscape gardeners of the eighteenth century, the idea of gardening was limited to the geometrically designed beds and borders known as 'knot gardens', which contained an assortment of perennials, bulbs, a few shrubs, and of course herbs for both culinary and medicinal use. In 1596 John Gerard published his *Catalogue* of plants growing in his garden near London, and this was one of the first books to draw attention to the new plants that were reaching northern Europe and especially England from the lands that were then being discovered and explored across the globe. It was at this time that gardening – in the sense of cultivating plants for their interest and ornamental value alone – really began.

Men were setting forth on the seas and returning with their ships laden with every sort of curiosity and treasure from abroad, and a mania developed for collecting any kind of object from the New World – including species of plant life. The problem of keeping plants in good condition during the long voyage home was solved by the invention of the Wardian Case by Nathaniel Ward. These miniature glasshouses – the forerunners of the terrarium – were kept on deck, and they let in light but retained moisture, thus preserving the plants from rough conditions and making them easier to handle. There was of course no problem with bulbs or seeds.

With the fashion for natural curiosities firmly established and the means of satisfying it invented, collectors began to form the famous 'cabinets' – cases full of weird and wonderful objects from abroad. The first recorded cabinet belonged to John Tradescant (1567–1637), who was gardener to Charles I. Tradescant was one of the first people to travel and explore specifically for the purpose of collecting plants, journeying widely through America, Russia, Europe and the Mediterranean seaboard. As well as a 'physic garden' full of rare plants, his cabinet contained collections of stuffed animals and birds, shells, minerals and fossils. The collections he passed on to his son, also John Tradescant (1608–1662), who succeeded his father as royal gardener – and it is obvious that he also inherited his father's interests. In 1657 he went to the new colony of Virginia to gather flowers, plants and shells to add to the collection at Lambeth, which had become known as the 'Ark'. It was on this journey that he discovered the border perennial *Tradescantia virginiana*.

One of the younger Tradescant's contemporaries was Sir Hans Sloane, who took it upon himself to rescue the physic garden in Chelsea which the apothecaries had founded. The term 'physic garden' – implying the cultivation of herbs for medicine – was by now a misleading one. As was evident from the Tradescants, plant collections at this time must have contained many plants other than herbs. These early collectors were, by virtue of their interest in plants *per se*, the founding fathers of gardening as we know it.

The vogue for botany and plant collecting went from strength to strength. One of the most notable eighteenth-century botanists was Sir Joseph Banks (1743–1820), who accompanied Captain Cook on his first voyage round the world. The journey made him appreciate just how infinitely rich was the world's flora and, when he later became director of Kew Gardens, inspired him to send many of the great plant hunters of his age out on their travels around the globe. Among them was Francis Masson (1741–1805), who discovered the lovely bird of paradise flower, *Strelitzia reginae*, and William Kerr (d. 1841), who found the Chinese bamboo *Nandina domestica*. Other collectors followed: the voyages of Sir Joseph Hooker (1817–1911) to the Himalayas enriched the rhododendrons; William Lobb (1809–63) went to South America where he found, amongst other things, the Chilean fire bush, *Embothrium coccineum*; meanwhile the Treaty of Nanking in 1842 at last opened up China to travellers and in that year Robert Fortune (1812–80) was sent there by the Royal Horticultural Society – he found many species, including *Mahonia japonica*.

The names of many other collectors live on in their plant discoveries. Père Jean-Marie Delavay found the lovely *Magnolia delavayi*; Père Armand

David discovered the pocket handkerchief tree, *Davidia involucrata*. Fortune's discoveries led others to the Far East. Ernest Henry Wilson brought back one of the richest harvests – over six hundred plants including *Lilium regale* and *Buddleia davidii*. George Forrest found three hundred new plants, many of which were rhododendrons, including *R. griersonianum*. Two more notable collectors who made a joint trip to China were William Purdom (1880–1921) and Reginald Farrer (1880–1920). Their expeditions were funded not only by institutions like Kew and by wealthy private individuals, but also by the great horticultural firms that grew up as interest in and demand for the new plants increased. Conrad Loddiges & Son of Hackney was one of the first suppliers of the new trees, shrubs, orchids and tender plants that were to reach their peak of popularity in Victorian times.

Great changes were also afoot in the field of garden design. Although knot gardens were no longer used exclusively for the cultivation of herbs by the eighteenth century, their highly patterned design still dominated the way the new plants were deployed. All this was to be swept away by the great landscape gardeners. Men like William Kent and Lancelot (Capability) Brown thought in terms of spacious lawns, rolling views over parkland studded with trees, ornamental lakes and grottoes with artfully ruined temples. Their radical revision of the meaning of the garden gave way at the beginning of the nineteenth century to the 'gardenesque'. This was influenced by Humphry Repton, and thereafter by the landscapers Nesfield and Barry, who had admired the Italian style of gardening and set about reviving the formal terraces, parterres and geometric shapes that previously dominated the scene. By around 1850 the flower bed itself had arrived, and it was used to incorporate many of the new tender and exotic plants that had recently been introduced and were being raised in ever-increasing numbers of greenhouses. Seeds for these bedding plants were largely supplied by Sutton & Sons and Thompson of Ipswich. But by the time the influx of new plant material had reached its peak the greatest name in horticulture was that of Veitch of Chelsea – William Lobb and E. H. Wilson were just two of the plant collectors in their employment. With the ever-increasing variety that became available, public interest continued to grow – and so did the number of nursery firms specializing in plants such as orchids, ferns, and exotic-leaved 'stove' plants.

This was the heyday of the greenhouse – so called because when introduced at the end of the seventeenth century they were used exclusively for the growing of green plants. In Victorian times they were often large and elaborate affairs, and were sometimes referred to as 'winter gardens' or as 'palm' or 'stove' houses, the stove being the apparatus used to heat them. The plants enjoyed the finest conditions for growth, and were cultivated on a scale and to a degree of perfection that has never been equalled. Every middle-class Victorian family could afford to run a greenhouse. Labour and especially heating were very cheap, and no expense was spared in maintaining whatever temperature was required – which in some cases was as high as a minimum of 70°F. Comparatively little was known of many of what were then new and highly exotic plants, and some of the species we now know to be hardy were cosseted in these steamy greenhouses. Camellias, for example, were one of the earliest occupants of the greenhouse, and were to remain there for decades, along with their many new companions.

Many greenhouses were also used for the mass cultivation of brightly coloured bedding plants for the fashionable 'carpet bedding' schemes of the day, but this was soon to change. A man arrived on the scene who was to have a profound effect on garden fashion and taste. His name was William Robinson, and he had very firm ideas and opinions about all aspects of gardening. He arrived in Britain from his native Ireland in 1861 to work for the Royal Botanic Society, devoting his spare time to writing. Six years later he was representing the horticultural firm of Veitch & Sons and *The Times* at the Paris Exhibition. Over the following years he wrote several books, the most important and effective of which was *The English Flower Garden*. First published in 1883, it has become a classic and is still reprinted to this day.

Robinson had a particular hatred for bedding schemes, especially the carpet bedding variety, which he considered to be outmoded and a waste of money and labour, and he led a ceaseless campaign against their deployment. He made no bones about his views in his writing, as this example shows:

> Bedding out or marshalling flowers in geometric patterns is a
> thing of our own precious time, and carpet bedding is simply a

Eucomis bicolor

further remove in ugliness . . . The beautiful forms of flowers are degraded to crude colour without reference to the natural forms or beauty of the plants.

He was certainly a man after my own heart – and, incidentally, his opinions concurred with those of Sir Francis Bacon, who wrote about the use of geometric patterns and colours in his 'Essay on Gardens' in 1625: 'Knots or figures with divers coloured earths be but toys. You may see as good sights many times in tarts.'

Robinson saw that with all the new plant species now available far more interesting, beautiful and tasteful gardens could be created at far less expense by using hardy plants. In his books he advocated using them in a totally informal and natural way, with a strong emphasis on plant character and individuality. Any kind of mass planting was dispensed with. In his book *The Wild Garden* of 1881, foliage too played an important part, especially that of the more exotic-looking plants. But in his little book *The Subtropical Garden* of 1871 he incorporated many subtropical and even tropical or 'stove' plants as subjects for planting out in the summer months (after a period of hardening off) in sheltered nooks or 'dells'. However, he was at pains to prevent people making the mistake (as some had done) of planting out the more delicate (and often expensive) stove plants: they may have looked decorative in the garden, but made no perceptible growth and sometimes died – an obviously pointless exercise. Most of the plants Robinson recommended were hardy, and when suggesting subtropical species he was careful only to include subjects which thrived outside in the summer months, making very substantial growth before the threat of frost necessitated their removal indoors.

Robinson's practical and economical approach to gardening was to seem all the more percipient after the turn of the century. The value of agricultural land was soon to halve and the great private gardens were to enter a slow demise, accelerated by the First World War. The extravagant bedding schemes seemed to be more and more inappropriate, and were to survive only in the great public parks. Robinson's style and ideas might not have been so popular had things been different, but at a time of recession his luck was in. He was to influence gardening for many years, and does so to this day, though not so much as I would like. He is now often referred to as the Father of English gardening.

With the disappearance of the great private greenhouses, many of the plants they had housed also disappeared from the scene, to remain only in very mild areas where they would survive out of doors. Others were to survive through the continued cultivation of tender plants for bedding out by parks departments – a system which continues to this day with, extraordinarily enough, many of the same plants – abutilons, cannas, ricinus, coleus, perilla, nicotiana, eucalyptus and cordyline amongst them. Little has changed, and huge expenditure is still made in growing them under glass, while vast numbers of man-hours are spent planting them out. It is ironic that a style of gardening which Robinson so disliked should play a part in saving some of the plants he loved from obliteration in this country. As well as the thousands of plants raised for the parks, some departments, notably the City of London, also grow a large stock of exotic species – crotons, palms, cordylines, and so on – for use as decoration at ceremonial occasions such as state banquets.

One of the finest examples of 'pleasure garden' plantings in Victorian times could be seen at Battersea Park – nowhere else in the country could subtropical bedding be seen on such a scale and with such a variety of plants. Even the great Abyssinian banana and similarly rare plants were on display. The longest possible period of growth was obtained by building raised beds on foundations of rubble or brick. These would catch and retain the sun's heat much more efficiently than the level ground, as well as providing the good drainage which many of these plants prefer. This is a particularly good method of growing plants which like to be 'baked' to encourage flowering, such as *Beschorneria yuccoides*. It must be said that the majority of the plants were grouped in ugly masses, which made even the most graceful of plants look clumsy, but, despite the unimaginative way in which they were deployed, it is a shame that these exuberant plantings are no longer to be seen. I for one would certainly prefer them to the boring and gloomy shrubberies that are usual nowadays.

Henry Cooke – The Man and His Book

•

Since the demise of exotic or subtropical gardening in Victorian times it has not, with a few exceptions, been practised up until the present day; and so far as I am aware I am the only person in this country indulging in it seriously. One of those exceptions, however, was a man who was gardening at the turn of the century and whose achievements in this field could not have been greater, making others' – including my own – seem modest by comparison. I speak, of course, of the man who was such an inspiration to me, Henry Cooke.

Few gardeners can have been as ambitious in their plans as this man, regardless of his good fortune, and what is more remarkable is the extent to which he was to achieve his ambitions.

While serving as Surgeon General in the Indian Army he would often dream of the house and garden he hoped to find back in England – ensconced in woody depths with lawns for tennis and croquet, gardens with water for ornament, and beautiful views of the surrounding countryside. Clearly his desires were not simple ones. Some years later he came upon William Robinson's book *The Wild Garden*, and from that moment he was determined that if he should have any garden at all it would be a wild one. Robinson advocated the use of mainly hardy exotic-looking plants, but Cooke's garden was to differ in the use of a large number of tender or subtropical ones. He had obviously admired the vegetation and the garden he had had while in India and Robinson's writings had further encouraged and confirmed his conviction that the wild garden was the perfect setting for subtropical plants.

On his retirement from office Cooke returned to England and began to search for the house and grounds he had dreamed of – but with little hope of finding his ideal. He was to visit many places in response to advertisements which now and then seemed promising, only to have his hopes dashed. Then, just as he felt that he would have to settle for something short of his requirements, he stumbled upon a site which was to exceed even his expectations.

It was in the most westerly part of Gloucestershire, beyond the River Severn and backed by the Forest of Dean. The hills rose to seven hundred feet and from their southern flank two tree-covered spurs extended to form a horse-shoe. In the deep recess of this valley stood the house and grounds, sheltered behind and on both sides by the hanging wood though still at the cool height of five hundred feet above the river. The site, exposed only to the south and south-west, got all the sunshine that was available and had magnificent views over the distant Cotswolds and the Severn. Below the terrace on which the house stood a little path through the woods led to an area of two acres enclosed with wire fencing. In this area were many fine trees, which one of Cooke's predecessors had planted some sixty years earlier, and three pieces of water on different levels, fed by a rivulet, which had been created by the same man. The top pool was a hundred yards long and curved in a U shape, enclosing an island. This pool overflowed into the second, from which a little stream replenished the bottom pond.

What more could anyone have wanted? It was a site and situation that any keen plantsman or gardener would have envied, and without which Cooke surely could not have succeeded.

On his arrival the area was neglected and overgrown and the only plants that had survived the ravages of time were hardy fuchsias and some coarser forms of hosta (then called funkia). Cooke first mended the fences and began clearing the brambles, gorse and bracken. He then added to the trees and conifers and set about the permanent planting of the garden. The course of the rivulet was diverted with moss-covered rocks and its margins planted with irises and lilies, including the giant *Cardiocrinum giganteum*, and along the paths hostas and astilbes. Clearings were made in the woods in which he planted bamboos and in between these leycesteria, eulalia, agapanthus, crinum, monbretia and arum lilies, etc. Cooke realized the importance of bamboos in forming the 'framework' of the subtropical garden and he was generous in their planting. He then planted the pond in this upper garden with water lilies and stocked it with trout. On the bank of the island he planted ligularias (then called senecios) and the bamboo *Sasa palmata*. Close by day lilies (*Hemerocallis*), ostrich ferns (*Struthiopteris*), shipper orchids (*Cypripedium*), and even the pitcher plant *Darlingtonia californica* were planted in hollows in the rocks.

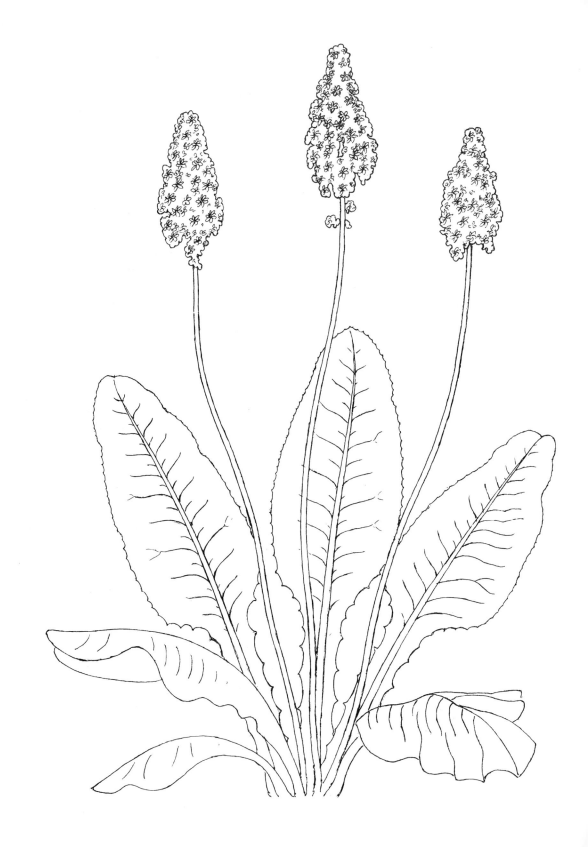

The lowest pond area was planted largely with polygonums and bamboos, and the spaces between the shrubs with rheums and eremuruses. However, it was the area around the middle pond that was to be Cooke's chief interest, and make the garden so exceptional. Here he planted the majority of the exotic plants. In 1877 he had built three great glasshouses, 25 feet high at one point, and a melon house with the most up-to-date method of heating, and these were to be taken full advantage of. In the area flanking the pond were permanent plantings of such things as phormiums, the palm *Trachycarpus* and yuccas, which in summer were supplemented with plants from the glasshouses – cannas, the ginger *Hedychium gardnerianum* with its orchid-like blooms, the rice paper plant *Tetrapanax papyriferus* (then called *Aralia papyrifera*), the datura with its white pendulous trumpet flowers (then called *Brugmansia knightii*), the sparmannia, and finally the banana *Musa ensete*, the Abyssinian banana, the most magnificent occupants of the garden.

The largest of these, which were some nine years old, were Cooke's proudest possession. 'I have seldom met with grander specimens of the banana even in India,' he wrote. 'The great fronds measure from twelve to fourteen feet in length and 2¾ feet in width and rise from the pedestal of the main stalk at a height of four feet from the ground so that they tower overhead to a total height of eighteen feet and are almost without a rent.' But to produce such magnificent specimens required shelter and huge amounts of water to compensate for the evaporation from the vast, sail-like leaves, 'under whose spreading arches an elephant might stand for shade,' and in hot weather the hose would be left on them for several hours at a time.

In other sheltered spots were planted the lovely Norfolk Island tree fern *Alsophila brownii* (then called *A. excelsa*) under the shade of the Mountain Ash, various other palms, and smaller specimens of the banana.

By now Cooke's dreams had been realized and, as he wandered through his garden admiring his surroundings, his thoughts would often turn to the garden he once tended in India. 'It only wants the gorgeous colouring of the magnificent Dracaenas, and the brilliantly painted leaves of

(Opposite) *Ligularia macrophylla*

the Crotons which attain to so great development in the Indian gardens to complete the picture,' he wrote.

Cooke's paradise garden was not without its problems, however. Rabbits, moles and mice would often gain entry, usually devouring the choicest and most expensive plants, and herons would persist in trying to steal the trout despite numerous attempts to discourage them. Cooke felt that if anyone was entitled to the trout it was he.

With the approach of autumn and the threat of frost came the great job of dismantling the garden, and despoiling it of its tender occupants. First to come up was the Norfolk Island tree fern, for it had the tenderest constitution; then the gingers, for, although they would have survived left *in situ* if protected, they would have been cut to the ground. The grevillea, the cannas, the rice paper plant, the datura and the sparmannia followed. Last came the bananas, as they were capable of withstanding a little more cold. The task of removing the largest of these proved in successive years to be an ever-increasing one. Cooke was fortunate in that he was able to call upon the assistance of six local men to lift and place them on a sledge, which would then be dragged the five or six hundred yards to the glasshouses by a team of horses hired from a neighbouring farm. It took them all day to lift the two largest plants, and in the autumn of 1899 Cooke decided as an experiment to leave one large musa out for the winter, wrapping its trunk and leaves with bracken and canvas, and placing iron sheets around its base to keep it dry. The splendid plant can never have looked so undignified. 'I confess it is a forlorn hope to expect that it may do well,' he wrote. 'The worst of our English climate is its uncertainty, and we in Gloucestershire are far worse off in the general run of our winters than the more favoured dwellers in distant Cornwall.'

But this was not to be the greatest of Cooke's anxieties. Like all devoted plantsmen and gardeners who pour so much of themselves into their creations, he often worried about the future of his garden both in terms of his old age and after:

> It sometimes troubles me when tending carefully the garden that I love, and which I think loves me (for there is certainly sympathy between us), to think that perhaps the same loving care will not be

lavished on it when I have ceased to possess it, and a doubt intrudes itself whether or no I may in the future state that is so soon approaching yet retain an interest in its welfare. Mundane things are so provokingly evanescent. But if our sympathies are still retained with the loved 'ones' we leave behind, why not with the loved 'things'.

Fortunately, Cooke and his garden were not to be obliterated by time, and powerful glimpses of it can be obtained from the pages and photographs of his book.

It is an interesting and sometimes amusing little book, the chapters on the garden and the plants interspersed with others devoted mainly to conversations between Cooke and two of his apparently most frequent visitors, the Professor and the Padre. We gardeners are often accused of being a trifle eccentric and it seems that Cooke was no exception. Here are a few pages from the beginning of one of these conversation chapters, entitled 'Odds and Ends'. They convey the charming and amusing – as well as interesting – character of the book.

A silvery laugh, perhaps a trifle too high-pitched, met us (the Professor and me) as we were going down the winding path to the garden, and as we turned a corner the Padre and the 'Daughter of the House' came into view. I thought that there was a slight flush on the check of the maiden and a somewhat corresponding hue on that of the Padre, who met us with hand outheld. 'I have been showing the Padre the Hedychium which is in flower, and we imagined that we might find you down there,' said the maiden, who thereupon left us, while the eye of the Padre followed the light-toned hues of the muslin gown as it vanished down the path. 'Ah! the Hedychium must be in grand flower just now,' said the Professor. 'It seems to have found a congenial home in the wild garden, and certainly it is in keeping with the exotics.' 'It belongs to a family that is truly exotic,' I said, 'and includes the Indian Shot (*Canna indica*), the lordly Alpinia, and the still grander Banana (*Musa*) and the Arrowroots (*Maranta arundinacea*) and the

Ginger (*Zingiber officinale*). I hope to try if the Alpinia will bear being planted out in the English summer, it was a charming addition to our Indian garden.' The wild ducks had heard my voice as we approached the little gate, and began their quacking from the recesses of the lower pond, for they recognise me by my voice, and when I whistled as we passed under the Deodar came flying up in a group, and plunged into the water with a swish that sent the little waves swirling up to the further bank, and the coquettish water hens, startled by the presence of strangers, scuttled across the water-lilies to the refuge of the island.

'The mallards have lost their magnificent plumage,' said the Professor. 'How queer they look disguised as the hen birds!' 'Yes indeed,' said I, 'they have discarded their marriage finery and assumed their every-day clothing, but they will don it again ere the winter begins. No doubt, it became dishevelled by their bickerings and fightings during the honeymoon time, and wanted renewing.'

'I wish the water-hens would come out,' said the Padre, 'I love to catch a glimpse of their charming movements and mincing ways as they deliberately plant their dainty feet and switch up their pretty tails in moving along. They are born coquettes, and air their whims and graces like one of their betters, only they have not a silvery laugh.' The Professor winked at me.

One day while I was pondering over this delightful book a great curiosity was aroused within me as to what had become of the garden. Nearly a century had passed and, although it obviously could not have survived the ravages of time intact, perhaps there was still a trace of its existence.

After some research I managed, to my amazement, to discover its exact location and its present owners, who had acquired the property about 1970. I contacted them and was subsequently invited to see the garden,

(Opposite) *Eremurus robustus*

though I was warned that I might be disappointed. These kindly people had bought the property, at first not knowing of the existence of the wild garden. On discovering it they took great interest in its origin and history and had begun work in trying to restore it to something of its former glory.

I arrived with a friend one summer day and we were warmly welcomed by our hosts, who were now living in another house on the site, having just moved from and sold the house which Cooke had occupied. After luncheon, over which it became apparent that our hosts had already formed some attachment for and pride in the garden, we were led by the lady of the house across the lawn and down onto a path in the woods leading to the wild garden. A strange air of expectancy overtook me as we drew close to the entrance where the little gate had been. On entering we were confronted with rampant armies of the great *Polygonum sachalinense* through which the owners had had to clear a path to gain entry, and which also hid from view (along with forests of the bamboo *Arundinaris japonica*) the lower pond. We were led through and up to the middle pond, the area which had once been the setting for Cooke's treasures, and the heart of the planting. Nothing remained of any of that – not unexpectedly – but for two fan palms (*Trachycarpus fortunei*) which towered above our heads almost into the tree tops, some rhododendrons, and a few other things which had stood the test of time. But still there was a great sense of atmosphere and, despite the trees' having grown beyond all proportion since Cooke's day, I was still able to recognize and visualize the garden as it must have been. For, after all, the essence of it was still there – the setting, the marvellous views, the water and the great forest trees.

Our host left us to peruse and explore at our leisure, and as I wandered, hoping to find some as yet undiscovered treasure, I thought for one brief moment that I heard a faint echo of that 'silvery laugh' that had filtered through those very trees so long ago, and I could not help but wonder as I gazed upon the forests of the polygonum: what if Cooke himself could see the garden now? What would his feelings be? Would they be a reflection of my own?

There is yet one more part to the story, which I have deliberately kept till last, and which I think Cooke would have approved of, though I beg his forgiveness for the assumption. A few years ago (1985, I think), the

Gunnera manicata

Musa ensete

Hedychium coccineum 'Tara'

Trachycarpus fortunei

owners were approached by a film company who undoubtedly knew of Cooke's story and who wished to film there, both in Cooke's original house and in the wild garden. Little did the owners realize it, but the garden was to experience a bigger upheaval than it had in Cooke's day. Tracks had to be made and a path cleared through the wood to make access for the vans and lorries of film equipment, and this necessitated the removal of many large trees. Holes were dug and exotic plants (including bananas) were brought in and planted, rather unimaginatively, around the garden. The film is the story of a widow, played by Deborah Kerr, struggling to maintain the garden that her husband had left, and the friendship she forms – somewhat cautiously – with a neighbour, an Indian lady, who helps her in the otherwise impossible task. The film is called *The Assam Garden*.

CHAPTER THREE

Designing and Creating an Exotic Garden

•

T he main problem with garden design is that it has become too architectural. Its tools are bricks and slabs and mortar and concrete rather than shrubs and trees and bags of peat. It is, of course, far easier to make man-made materials fit into design concepts, for plants have their own design and their own ideas about how to grow. If a garden is little more than an exercise in paving and brickwork, then the plants have to be pruned and trained and cut to size. The result is likely to be contrived and constrained, hardly a relaxing environment in which to rest from our labours and escape into a more peaceful world. A garden is, of course, a contrivance, but if successful it should contrive to look natural and informal, because this is the character of the materials we are dealing with. Few would disagree that a garden in which you feel as if you might be ensconced in a green clearing in the depths of the countryside (even if you are actually in the middle of a city) is much to be desired. Of course I am not suggesting that you should have to grapple with brambles and gorse; it is the effect we are aiming for.

The kind of plants recommended in this book would look totally out of place in a formal garden with borders and beds, especially if geometric in any way. The informal garden is the right and natural setting for them, and the obliteration of any straight lines is a prerequisite of designing an exotic garden. With the possible exception of terracing by the house, the exotic garden is a place of curves and contrasts, of differences in size, shape, texture and colour, of surprising perspectives, of drama and mystery and magic.

The Framework or 'Bones' of the Exotic Garden

•

When planting a garden it is good practice to think of the plants as consisting of four layers: the trees and shrubs form layers one and two while herbaceous plants and ground cover plants form layers three and four.

The trees and shrubs form the 'bones' of the garden, and in the case of the exotic garden these include large subjects such as bamboos and phormiums, which being evergreen also play an important role in winter. Trees are essential in any garden. They break up the skyline and ensure that your garden does not end abruptly five or six feet off the ground. The shade they cast is not only vital for many lower-growing plants, it also produces attractive dappled effects and contrasts of light and dark. Shrubs, apart from their inherent qualities, soften or hide boundaries of brick and fencing, and when suitably placed help to create different areas in the garden – which in its turn contributes to the element of mystery which the most enjoyable gardens always possess. The herbaceous plants supply the bulk of the flowers, while ground cover plants fill in the gaps lower down and have invaluable weed-suppressing qualities. Thus all four layers are of great importance in a well balanced garden.

It is most important that the framework (layers one and two) is planned and planted from the outset, especially when creating a garden from scratch. Although a garden is bound to change over the years, moving large trees and shrubs is both risky – as far as the chances of survival are concerned – and very disruptive for the rest of the garden, since plants adapt themselves to prevailing conditions and will not appreciate the sudden loss of shade or shelter. Given that the scheme you choose at the outset will probably be with you for some time, it is worth playing around with different layouts on paper before committing yourself.

Obviously both the trees and the hedging will take a number of years to develop. Average nursery specimens of trees are usually from 6 to 8 feet tall – sometimes less, sometimes more, depending on the subject. Some of the smaller trees are quite slow-growing and it may be six years before they become a developed feature, while some of the larger trees will reach the same state in only three or four years. Large specimen trees of some of the more common varieties are sold by some firms, but, apart from being very expensive, occasionally they will not establish themselves as well as younger or smaller specimens. Indeed, some species have to be planted in their final position when young as they will not take being moved at all.

The number of trees you plant will obviously depend on the size of your garden. Remember to take into account the size of the trees when fully developed, and also consider the amount and quality of shade they will cast and the amount you require for the other plants you want to grow. Much will depend on which way your garden faces, as trees will inevitably ration the amount of sun your garden gets. As a general rule of thumb, the hardy exotics described in Chapter Five are happy in sun or dappled shade, while the tender exotics – with the exception of the tree fern *Dicksonia antarctica*, which also likes dappled shade – prefer full sun. Finally, owners of small or dark gardens should not be deterred from growing one or two trees. There are plenty of small trees to choose from, as well as ones with an open habit or light foliage which cast much less shadow, such as eucalyptus or cercidophyllum.

Hedging must also be considered at the same time as trees, and a separate section on appropriate plants for creating boundaries round the exotic garden follows on page 47. It is obviously important, especially if the garden is in an exposed position, that hedging is established as quickly as possible, so as to provide shelter for those plants which require it.

Once you have laid out the trees and hedging, the final element of the framework to consider is that provided by the main shrubs, and in this case the bamboos and perhaps phormiums. The stronger shrubs will help to provide shelter as well as the hedging, so the sooner they are in position the better. As with trees, it is important to bear in mind the eventual size of the shrub before finally deciding where it should be positioned.

An attractive shrub is a feature in itself and should be given due prominence and space to grow. The bamboos are particularly striking and appropriate plants for the exotic garden, but remember that they do need a sheltered position – as do phormiums. Both these plants make a stunning

Sasa palmata

centrepiece around which to wind a path, or with which to create different areas in the garden.

It is worth bearing in mind that, while other plants come and go with the seasons, evergreens will be with you all the year round, and will be particularly important in winter. For this reason it is generally unwise to leave any area of the garden entirely bare of them.

Filling Out the Framework

•

A common failing in gardeners is that they grow a large variety of only a few plants – roses, for instance. This is a pity because restricting the number of different plants also restricts the range of effects of colour, shape, size and texture that can be achieved, as well as making it difficult to keep the garden looking interesting and beautiful for more than a few months of the year. Surely one of the greatest pleasures of gardening is that different plants give of their best at different times of year. With its wide diversity of leaf, flower and form the exotic garden is particularly rewarding from this point of view.

However, in very small gardens there is obviously a limit to the number of different plants that can be accommodated and careful selection is needed. It is worth bearing in mind that both the individual charms of a given plant and the overall effect of a garden can be ruined by bitty and fragmented planting. If too many plants are mixed in one small area the effect is of a mass of undistinguished growth in which nothing stands out. Scattered planting is thus both monotonous and uninspiring to look at, even when dealing with the most handsome subjects. If a plant is worth growing, then cultivate a respectable clump or area of it, and don't dot it round the garden where it will be lost. With most herbaceous species it is good practice, even in a small garden, to plant in threes, and this is particularly true of foliage plants – their attractions are often more subtle and they need to be planted boldly to show their full beauty. Obviously this would not be feasible with something like a gunnera in a small space – one plant would be enough to create an eye-catching effect. My garden is only forty by twenty feet, but *Gunnera manicata* was one of the first plants I ever grew. It is still there today and I have never had any desire to get rid of it.

Many people seem to be somewhat fearful of large plants, which is strange. It seems to me that with herbaceous plants in particular it is more important to grow species one admires – even if they do take up half the garden, they will give more pleasure to the gardener than a dozen less dramatic plants. Herbaceous plants may be divided if they become intrusive; and even one of the very largest plants recommended in Chapter Five, the banana *Musa ensete*, can easily be replaced by younger specimens, if it gets too big, since it is grown from seed. Obviously there will be limitations and no one in their right mind would, for example, plant a plane tree unless they had a garden the size of a park, for it could easily reach a hundred feet in a lifetime. But the all too prevalent tendency to behead anything that grows over six feet seems equally absurd. Plants naturally look their best when grown freely.

The list of plants in this book concentrates heavily on foliage, but by no means to the exclusion of flowers. It is lush foliage that makes a garden look exotic, especially that of the tender exotics. Many of the plants listed possess both beautiful foliage and flowers, but where a plant has been included for its flowers alone this is because it yields blooms that are exotic in appearance, and will therefore mix well with the foliage. Some lilies, for example, have this quality and to my mind look far more attractive in the informal setting of the exotic garden than in a traditional border.

With the proviso that every plant is given sufficient area and grown in sufficient quantities to distinguish itself, the exotic garden is most characterful when contrasting foliage shapes and colours (but not too many) are placed side by side – some suggestions are made in the descriptions of individual plants. There are some stunning combinations: the glaucous, grey, serrated leaves of *Melianthus major* and the purple spear-shaped leaves of *Canna generalis* 'Wyoming', for example, or the huge, round, pale green leaves of *Rodgersia tabularis* with the star-shaped bronze leaves of *Rodgersia podophylla*. But the possibilities are endless and it is fun to experiment, and with herbaceous plants mistakes are easily rectified. The exotic garden lends itself to this kind of playful approach. There are no formal patterns which have to be kept intact and surprises are welcome. Even the old rule about placing the shortest plants at the front and the tallest at the back can be reversed occasionally, so long as nothing is completely hidden from view. There is no reason, for example, why something like a ligularia should not be placed at the front of a border with, say, a hosta on a raised area behind it.

Colour

•

Colour will always be popular in the garden and it is the main attraction of flowers, but in their love for brilliant effects many gardeners have strayed from nature's way of displaying beauty. In nature bright colours are always set against an abundance of green (they are intended to attract attention, and what better way of doing so?) and colours seldom clash. The majority of popular garden flowers are the creation of hybridists and are too often over-sized and brash in colour, bearing little resemblance to their natural relatives.

There is a great misconception that foliage lacks colour, and is therefore boring and only suitable for filling in the gaps. In fact, herbaceous plants, shrubs and even trees are often superbly coloured. Purple is rich in the shrubs *Cotinus coggyria* 'Royal Purple' and *Corylus* 'Maxima Purpurea'. Bright yellow is abundant in foliage, especially the shrubs *Sambucus racemosa* 'Plumosa Aurea' and *Corylus avellana* 'Aurea', and in the tree *Robinia pseudoacacia* 'Frisia'. Variegation of white, cream and yellow is also widespread, and even pink variegation is to be found in the shrub *Fagus sylvatica* 'Roseo-marginata' and pink and white in the climber *Actinidia kolomitka*. The shrubs *Pieris formosa* 'Forest Flame' and *Pieris formosa forrestii* 'Wakehurst' have brilliant red new foliage which slowly turns to cream and then green.

It is important to have a colour scheme in a well designed garden, though there are no hard and fast rules to follow. Generally people group too many colours together, some of which do not harmonize. No interior designer would use more than three colours when decorating a room, and the same should be true of any one area in the garden. Apart from limiting the number of colours, there is one personal preference I have, which is for mixing purple-foliaged plants with white rather than yellow variegated species. I feel that yellow is a more suitable companion for the warmer colours, such as oranges and reds.

There will always be those who strive for as much colour as possible in the garden, but it is interesting that many people turn in later life to the more restful hues and many and various shapes of foliage – this is certainly true of some of our most famous gardeners. Whether it is because they have gained greater knowledge of the effects that can be achieved without flowers playing a central role, or whether it is simply that they don't want to have to work quite so hard on their gardens, I do not know – perhaps it is both. Cost may be another factor, for no type of gardening could be more expensive to maintain than a border full of annuals requiring several replantings a year.

What Plants To Grow?

•

Whatever part of the country you live in, an exotic effect can be achieved in the garden, but for the best results local conditions have to be taken into account. It is difficult to generalize, since frost traps or pockets of warmth can occur almost anywhere. But if you live in the Midlands or the North it would be advisable to concentrate on the hardy exotics, simply because the period when you will be able to grow the tender exotics out of doors may be frustratingly short. For those in the south and west a mixture of both hardy and tender subjects would be appropriate, with the tender plants forming about 30 per cent of the total. People living in the very mild areas of

Cornwall, southern Ireland and the west coast of Scotland could devote their gardens entirely to tender plants, providing they have adequate shelter from winds. I think, however, that to restrict one's choice entirely to tender plants would be a trifle boring – and even in the mildest areas it is also a little risky, since a single spell of extreme weather could destroy the garden completely.

Boundaries, Screens and Hedges

•

For most people the boundaries of the garden will prove the most obstinate obstacle in the way of banishing straight lines from the scene. Existing walls and fences are the trickiest in this respect, and the best solution, especially in small gardens, is to concentrate on disguising them with climbers and a few evergreen shrubs. Corners can be softened with bamboos or small trees as well as shrubs, and subjects such as mahonia look good with a background and benefit from the shelter, especially the rather tender *Mahonia lomarifolia*. This shelter is valuable to other plants, too, but remember that shrubs, especially evergreens, also give protection. For the intervening gaps, climbers should be used. Ivies are some of the best for quick cover and have the added advantage of being evergreen, but they should be broken up with other plants such as the occasional deciduous climber or shrub as large areas of ivy look gloomy. Trellis panels can be fixed to the top of the wall or fence, and will provide extra height for climbers without casting too much shade. If you are stuck with too much brickwork it is certainly an advantage to be able to grow plants high enough to obscure surrounding buildings and help create a feeling of seclusion, of a private haven.

Undoubtedly a hedge is the best form of boundary in an exotic garden. Hedges offer scope for the kind of informal variation appropriate to the plants they surround, and they also filter the wind – unlike solid barriers, which tend to produce turbulence. Hedges are far more attractive when they consist of an assortment of plants – only in formal gardens do they need to be composed of a single species. Using a variety of plants produces an irregular and thus informal margin as the different plants grow to different heights and widths, which they should be allowed to do.

Before planting any new hedging material give the soil a dressing of manure and bonemeal, and an addition of peat if conditions are dry. New hedges will require staking in the first year – either the plants can be staked individually or posts be set six feet apart with wire stretched between them to which the plants can be tied. Once the hedge is established, the posts and wire can be removed, but this may be unnecessary as they will most probably be entirely hidden from view. The rate of growth of different hedging plants varies, but a reasonable hedge can be grown in three or four years. It then only needs to be complemented by one or two other shrubs to complete the job. Remember that when starting a garden from scratch the hedge is one of the very first things to plant.

If you already have a hedge it will undoubtedly be of one type of shrub, and probably of monotonous appearance. Any unattractive hedge can be enhanced by clematis of various kinds, which will ramble over it and even up into trees. Alternatively, existing hedges can be turned into more informal boundaries by removing sections of them and filling the gaps with other hedging plants. Remember that the ground where the sections of the old hedge have been removed will probably be starved of nutriment.

As is well known, the fastest growing of all hedging plants is the Lawson or Leyland cypress, but in my opinion its rate of growth is the only point in its favour. These cypresses look both formal and dismal, and should be used only for screening round tennis courts and suchlike. All of the plants listed below will eventually make a hedge from six to ten feet high, and in large gardens where space permits they will grow even taller if allowed – in this case they are simply grown as very large shrubs and are usually referred to as screens. It is important to decide in advance how high you want the hedge to be: the greater the desired height, the greater the width the hedge will require.

When the trees and shrubs in the garden are given a top dressing of fertilizer (every one or two years), the hedge should be included. Clipping will not be necessary so often as with a formal hedge, being required only to

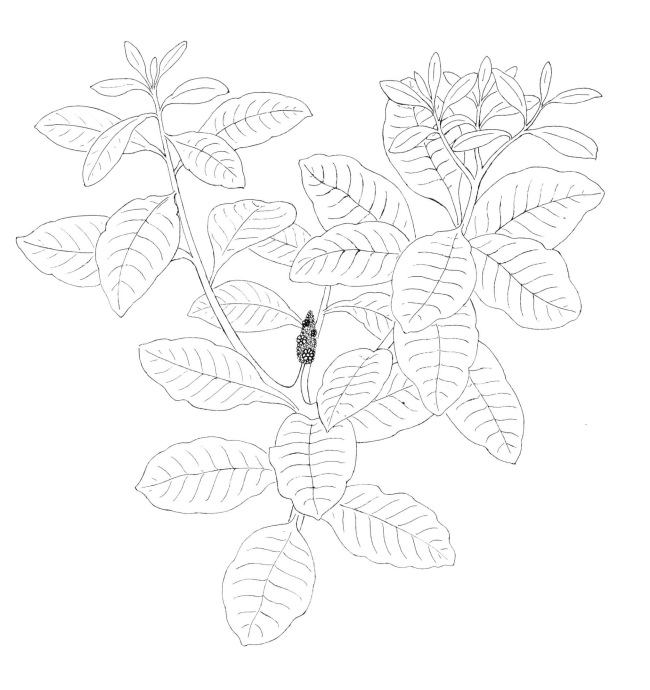

Phytollaca clavigera

keep the hedge within the desired bounds. Never clip large-leaved hedging plants such as cherry laurel with shears – it disfigures the foliage – but prune them with secateurs.

Evergreen hedges are obviously preferable in some ways to deciduous ones – they are attractive all year round and give better wind protection. But hedges of the popular beech and hornbeam, though deciduous, have the advantage of retaining their dead leaves through the winter, which improves the quality of the protection they afford. All of the following plants have the most important characteristic of forming a close network of leaves and branches from ground level upwards.

Prunus lusitanica (Portugal laurel)

I consider this to be one of the most handsome of all hedging plants. The glossy evergreen leaves have reddish stalks, and in summer this plant produces slender spikes of small, white, scented flowers which are followed by purple-black cherries.

Prunus laurocerasus (cherry laurel)

This evergreen shrub is similar to the Portugal laurel but is of altogether larger proportions in leaf and flower and is of less refined habit. It produces erect spikes of creamy white flowers in late spring.

Eleagnus × *ebbingei*

This rapid-growth shrub soon forms an impenetrable barrier of its medium-sized evergreen leaves, which are silvery underneath. In October it bears little white clove-scented flowers.

Cotoneaster × *watereri* 'Cornubia'

This small-leaved semi-evergreen shrub has stems that arch outwards in maturity. In late spring small creamy flowers appear, followed by a mass of bright-red berries.

Prunus cerasifera 'Pissardii' (purple-leaved cherry)

It is nice to give variety to a hedge with a change in foliage colour as well as size or shape. This plant is more usually seen as a small standard tree, but it makes a lovely hedge. The medium oval deciduous leaves are red-purple when young but mature to a dark purple in summer. Before the leaves unfold it has pale purple blossoms, which are later followed by reddish plums.

Fagus sylvatica 'Purpurea' (purple beech)

This is not quite as vigorous as the plain green form but is much more attractive. The colour is variable but is usually a darkish purple.

Carpinus betulus (common hornbeam)

A common sight along country lanes, the hornbeam has leaves of similar size, shape and colour to the common beech. In spring, yellowish male and green female catkins appear, and in late summer little ribbed nuts are formed.

Paths

•

Paths partly dictate the shape of a garden and therefore their positioning is of great importance.

It never fails to astonish me that so many gardens (admittedly usually long and straight) possess perfectly straight paths, usually leading to nowhere but the garden shed. True, many gardeners inherit such paths with the garden, but many still build them. In an informal garden especially, the path should wind and twist, providing an element of mystery which is heightened by the use of shrubs or clumps of bamboo to make it impossible to take in the entire garden, or the entire extent of the path, at a single glance. If you can see clearly what lies at the end of the path, why should you want to follow it? A well positioned shrub will draw the eye down the path, and if the path winds round it then an element of curiosity about what lies beyond will always be present. In addition, a good-sized shrub positioned in the bend of your path will make it look as if the path had to deviate to get round it. Such a scheme will add maturity to the appearance of the garden, and the path will seem to be a natural way through the vegetation, rather than an imposition upon it.

Clever positioning of a path can also give a false impression of the shape or size of your garden. Wind the path back and forth from side to side so that it exploits the width of the garden to the full and a narrow garden will appear to be broader. Double a path back upon itself and the garden will seem to have hidden depths and a more interesting shape – so long as you conceal one part of the path from the other with a screen of shrubs.

Varying levels add interest in the same way, breaking up a dull perspective and discouraging the eye from following a predictable line. Unfortunately, this is difficult to achieve in a flat garden where large amounts of earth would have to be moved, though it is certainly worth thinking about if you are starting from scratch and have some able-bodied help with the earthworks. In a garden which already slopes, steps can form a feature and emphasize the different levels. In large gardens old railway sleepers make very attractive steps and are cheaper than stone. Grow a bold plant such as rheum on one side to make them a more distinctive feature and also to soften their edges. Of course, any steps should incorporate the path at some point and this has to be taken into account in planning the garden.

Paths should be at least four feet wide – sufficient for two people walking side by side. Any wider and it will be difficult to snake the path through a small garden; and only in gardens which have to cope with large numbers of people are wider paths necessary. Besides, the closer the vegetation to the path, the greater the sense of mystery it will evoke.

York paving is still probably the best and most attractive material to use, but it is very expensive. However, simulated types of stone paving, made of reconstituted stone, are now available; they are much cheaper and come in a variety of colours. One thing I am totally against is the cementing together of paving stones, whether for paths or terracing. I feel it quite spoils the finished appearance. Providing the slabs are properly laid on a good foundation, preferably topped with sand, it is quite unnecessary to cement them. The gaps between them can be filled with fine gravel, which will look far more attractive and help to drain away surface water, thus preventing the formation of algae which can make them dangerously slippery. A few weeds may come up but these can easily be controlled by a path weed killer. Gravel is a pleasant material for paths, but loose gravel is uncomfortable to walk on and is inclined to get scattered everywhere. A three-inch-thick bed of cement should be laid on a foundation of fine rubble and a layer of gravel – or, better still, pea shingle – scattered on the wet cement. Remember to make the surface slightly bowed to allow the water to drain off. In small gardens old bricks make attractive paths, especially if they extend from a terrace of the same material. Avoid using the yellow ones, however, as they can be destroyed by frost. Cement will have to be used here to strengthen and hold them together, but providing it is brushed well into the crevices it will not be offensive.

Water and Water Features

·

Nothing adds so much to a garden as water: to begin with, life, interest, and beauty. It is attractive in any volume, from a tiny pool to a vast lake. Its presence enlarges the scope and variety of plants that can be grown, and a wealth of subjects which add a unique lushness and fertility to the garden cannot be grown without it. But it is the sound and movement of water, such as from a cascade or waterfall, that adds the final complement, bringing tranquility to the scene and creating a peaceful, almost romantic atmosphere. Introducing water is certainly one of the easiest ways of achieving those most desirable of qualities in the garden: magic and mystery. One may wonder whence the water is coming or where it is going, or come upon an unexpected 'secret' pool in shade, or a breathtaking waterfall sparkling in the sunlight, or a gently meandering stream coiling its way between moss-covered rocks. Water is such a versatile element, always creating interest, and it should always form the main area of interest or focal point even in the exotic garden, where the vegetation plays a strong and dramatic role.

It is neither difficult nor expensive to introduce water into the garden and owners of small gardens should not feel inhibited about having it. Gone are the days when creating a pool or pond was a long and arduous business involving the use of much cement. Pond liners now make it possible to make even a large pond in as little as a day. I am deliberately omitting to discuss prefabricated ponds, as these are always difficult to disguise and their shapes are usually so ugly.

Pond liners basically come in two types of material: PVC and butyl rubber. Butyl liners are around twice the price of PVC but are much longer lasting (usually eighty years). PVC liners vary in thickness, and the thinner ones should be avoided as they will puncture or damage too easily.

Making a Pool

•

aving decided what size and shape of pool you want (avoiding regular shapes such as circles or ovals), mark out its boundaries with short lengths of bamboo cane. With large ponds especially, there will be a substantial amount of soil to dispose of from the digging, so decide beforehand what is to be done with it. It is often desirable to have a raised area at the back of the pool, so some can be used here. Remember too that you will need a quantity of soil for marginal beds, but this should have some good new soil incorporated into it.

Dig the hole six inches deeper than your planned water depth: the liner will need to be covered with several inches of shingle or loam. A depth of about two feet is quite sufficient for most ponds. Avoid making the sides too steep or they will tend to collapse. When all necessary soil has been removed go over the area with a rake to level it and remove any stones (with large ponds it would be better to use a roller). Then cover the whole pond area with two inches of sand, which forms a good base for the liner. Lay out the liner, secure it in several places around the edge with rocks or bricks and begin to fill with water from a hose. As the pond fills most of the creases in the liner can be smoothed out; the weight of the water will assist in this. When the pond is almost full, turn off the hose and cut away the bulk of the surplus liner material, and then check the soil level around the pond and see that it corresponds with that of the water. Tuck the surplus edge of the liner down into the soil and bury it.

Finally, cover the liner with three or four inches of pea shingle or heavy loam so that it is completely hidden. The introduction of this material should bring the water level up to the desired height.

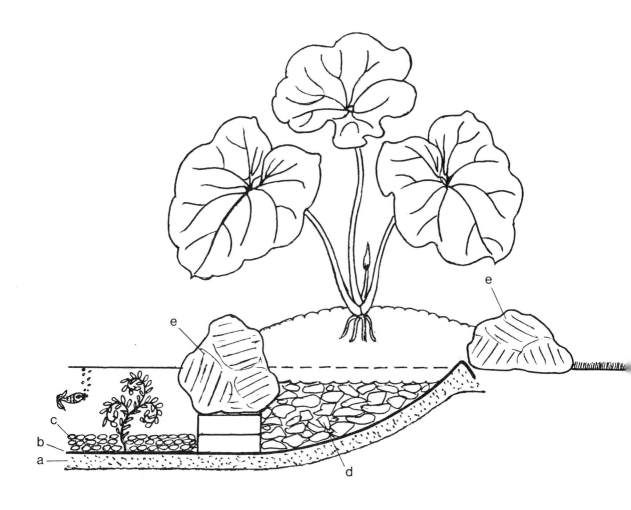

Section of a pond and marginal bed, showing: *a*, layer of sand; *b*, liner; *c*, layer of shingle; *d*, drainage material (rocks or rubble); *e*, rocks for retaining the soil in the marginal beds – the bricks simply enable smaller rocks to be used for this purpose. The outer rocks are not essential and turf can be laid right up to the edge of the liner if preferred.

These marginal beds need not encircle the pond completely, but can form pockets for planting at intervals around the edge, which would be a more appropriate way of treating a small pond

Marginal Beds

•

All but the smallest of ponds will be able to accommodate these beds, which are inside the perimeter of the pond liner (see illustration on p.56). They provide constantly moist or boggy conditions for the plants that require them, such as astilbes, bog primulas, peltiphyllum, osmunda, and so on.

Marginal beds should be built on a foundation of six inches of draining material so that most of the soil is above water level. In this way the plants receive sufficient moisture without the soil being unnecessarily waterlogged – the soil will soak up the water and the roots of the plants can work their way down to it. Use a heavy loam – it will not wash into the pond as will a loose and friable one – and eventually the roots of the plants will bind the soil together. Rocks are best for retaining the soil, and they give an attractive and natural look to the pool, especially when they become covered in mosses. They will also provide continuity if there is a cascade built of the same material.

Because of their size and depth of root, two plants are unsuitable for the marginal beds of artificial pools: lysichiton and gunnera. Lysichitons are very small when purchased and although they take many years to mature they are ultimately very large and deep-rooted plants. They very much resent disturbance once established and should be planted for life. Gunneras, on the other hand, can reach their full and very large size in two or three years, but if moved will settle down after a year or so.

The best method of growing these two plants with artificial ponds is to dig a pit alongside the pool. This should be lined with PVC sheeting in which a few holes have been made for drainage. Then place a layer of rubble or broken brick over the bottom of the pit to a depth of around six or eight inches, and fill up the pit with good rich soil to a depth of eighteen inches (to about six inches above water level). Arrange it so that the water from the pool overflows into this area or seeps into it from the margin. These are the only two plants that need to be treated in this way.

Aquatic and Other Plants

•

Marginal aquatics are best grown in baskets in the shallower parts of the pond. Avoid growing too many plants which tend to be very vigorous (water lilies, for example); in a short time they may completely cover the surface of the water, destroying the beauty of the pool. This is a common mistake. One of the chief purposes of having a pond is the sight of water and it is a crime to hide it with a carpet of green. It would be more agreeable to install some fish, which are far more eye-catching. Lush planting around the perimeter of the pool will appear to reduce its size somewhat as some of the leaves of these plants will naturally hang over it, and so the pool should be made as large as can be accommodated. Remember that fish need well oxygenated water, so include some good oxygenating plants in your scheme – these will also help to keep the water clear.

Cascades, Waterfalls and Their Construction

•

Natural-looking water features are by far the loveliest in informal gardens and the most enchanting of these is the waterfall. Ordinary fountains suit the formal surroundings associated with terraces and geometric pools but look quite out of place anywhere else, and the trickle of a fountain cannot be compared to the splashing of a waterfall – an important consideration if one wishes to muffle any external sounds, such as traffic. Certainly for effect a waterfall is about the most dramatic of water features one could have in an informal garden and a carefully built one surrounded by an attractive planting would be the envy of all one's neighbours. The larger the garden then obviously the larger or taller the waterfall can be, but even a small garden can contain quite an impressive drop.

The first and most important consideration is siting. The waterfall should be placed so that it looks attractive not only from the garden but from the house as well if possible; and if it can be arranged that the falling water catches the sunlight, so much the better. When buying the rock choose the most weathered blocks, so that the structure will not look too new when it is completed. Try to make the blocks of stone look like a natural outcrop of rock by laying them so as to give an impression of strata or layers of rock. Incorporate little pockets here and there in the structure for planting ferns and suchlike, which will help to make the whole feature softer and more mature in appearance.

Waterfalls which consist of one sheer drop are usually more beautiful than stepped cascades because the fall of water is more dramatic. However, a crashing waterfall might not be desirable, especially in a small garden, where the gentle splashing of a cascade may be preferred. A small pool at the top of the cascade, overflowing down into the pond, will provide a reasonably wide fall. A fibreglass mould is probably best for this; it will not be visible if the waterfall is a reasonable height and it is more easily arranged among the rocks. Special waterfall pumps which can circulate the necessary volume of water are readily available from good garden centres. An important point to remember is that water should be pumped into the rear of the top pool.

Problems very often arise in trying to achieve a clear drop of water from the ledge at the front of the top pool, as water will tend to cling to the face of the rock. The ledge should be completely flat on its upper surface and project at least six inches from the face of the rock below. If this still does not produce the desired effect then the problem can be overcome by fixing a sheet of clear perspex on top of the ledge, projecting an inch or two at the front. This will produce a perfect curtain of water and will not be visible.

Streams

•

In a large garden a stream can be a very beautiful feature. It may connect two pools and be crossed at one point by a path over a little bridge or a simple plank if the stream is very small. The butyl supplied for pools can also be obtained by the yard in varying widths and is ideal for making streams. It should be laid in exactly the same way as when making a pool. Needless to say, the stream should curve and twist just as it would if it were a natural one, and rocks can be used again – this time simply to break the regularity of the banks of the stream and perhaps occasionally to create pockets of soil for moisture-loving plants. Shingle or smooth pebbles make an attractive covering for the bottom of a small stream, while cobblestones and boulders will make the water flow prettily if a broader channel can be accommodated. It is far better if the stream is flowing as this keeps the water crystal clear. This can be achieved by running the stream between two ponds on slightly differing levels, with a pump to take the water back to the higher pond.

Sculpture, Stonework, Urns and Seating

•

It became very fashionable in Victorian times to use statuary and stonework in large informal gardens. The pieces ranged from simple architectural fragments (most probably rifled from ruins during trips abroad) to man-made follies such as pavilions, towers and ruined temples – as can be seen in many of the great gardens around the country.

The use of statuary in the exotic garden, however, is rather limited. In the first place, it is often prohibitively expensive. In the second place, only reasonably large and striking (and therefore even more costly) pieces will be able to hold their own with the bold foliage of many of the exotics, and nothing is sillier than a piece of stonework that is dwarfed or even hidden by a simple shrub. Finally, most sculpture is better associated with terracing, steps and walls rather than isolated in the garden. As with all elements in the design of an exotic garden, the plants themselves take priority, so that any piece which does not blend with them should be avoided.

In general, anything heavy, angular, geometric or 'static' will not suit the exotic garden. The choice of items is obviously very much a matter of personal opinion, but it seems to be that Italian Baroque pieces associate well with exotic vegetation because of their fluidity and the element of the fanciful they often contain. Sculpture with a Gothic flavour may also add a witty element to the garden, and also a touch of magic, however grotesque. Such pieces often associate well with water – gargoyles, of course, are designed to do so. More important, every piece should look old and weathered, so that it blends with its surroundings and looks as if it has been in place for many years. New pieces can be made to look old by encouraging mosses and lichens to grow over them – this happens naturally in damp and shady conditions, but can otherwise be encouraged by pouring water in which rice has been boiled over them. Plants should be allowed to ramble over them, giving the impression of a ruin overtaken by jungle or of an abandoned garden. Building fragments in the early Greek style, if one can find them, can create this effect particularly well.

Siting is obviously of critical importance – pieces must make a striking impression. A piece should either be situated in an obvious but dramatic position to which the eye is naturally drawn, or it should be a feature you come across unexpectedly as you turn a corner – perhaps a figure partially marked by a shrub. The real problem with siting statuary in the exotic garden is that wherever it goes it must look as if it has been casually placed rather than meticulously positioned. The only way to achieve this is to experiment with several different positions.

Some form of seating is obviously a must in any garden. Ideally it will be in the most attractive and interesting part of the garden, and as such it is likely to be facing a focal point or feature, such as water. Stone seats or benches (especially curved ones) look far more appealing than anything else placed among lush vegetation. Of course the price generally dictates what kind of seating is used, but it would be a shame to spoil a beautifully planted and grown exotic garden with ugly furniture.

Ornamental urns and other decorative plant containers (preferably stone again) are often delightful objects in themselves, but again are best confined to the terrace or patio. They are ideally placed on either side of steps and look very bold and characterful when planted up with plants such as cordylines, especially the purple *Cordyline australis* 'Atropurpurea'.

Some Basic Layouts

•

For those who wish to set about building an exotic garden, I hope that the following suggested plans for gardens of different sizes will show how unusual and enjoyable effects can be achieved with the use of exotic-looking plants. The planting is naturally dictated by the size of the garden, but the following suggestions aim to show how a small garden can become an excitingly exotic place.

There is no need to follow these suggestions religiously – part of the point of an informal garden is that it gives free rein to individual tastes. But I would emphasize that you should endeavour to keep your gardens, whatever the layout, looking as natural and uncontrived as possible.

You will notice that all my designs include water. I have made my feelings clear as to why I think every garden should have it: it is like a car – if you have never had one you don't miss it, but once you have had one it becomes a necessity. Far better in my view to go without a patio or terrace and have a pool instead. Sitting by water, even if it is only on a simple bench, is always delightful.

Two suggested layouts for gardens around forty feet long

1. Sasa palmata
2. Lysichitum americanum
3. Eucalyptus pauciflora
4. Ligularia 'Desdemona'
5. Peltipayllum peltatum
6. Fatsia japonica
7. Primula florindae
8. Arundinaria murielae
9. Rodgersia podophylla
10. Datua cornigera
11. Musa ensete
12. Pieris formosa 'Wakehurst'
13. Rheum tanguticum
14. Arundinaria nitida
15. Trachycarpus fortunei
16. Hosta sieboldiana elegans
17. Phormium tenax
18. Cercidophyllum japonicum
19. Acanthus mollis latifolius

Small Gardens (Under Fifty Feet Long)

•

The smaller the garden, the more selective you should be in your choice of plants, but I would recommend a heavy concentration on evergreens as bareness is more apparent in small gardens during the winter months. You could perhaps have the hardy palm *Trachycarpus fortunei* instead of a tree. Some other essentials, which would be very much in keeping with this palm, would be the smaller bamboo, *Arundinaria nitida* or *Arundinaria murieliae*, the New Zealand flax *Phormium tenax* and the shrub *Fatsia japonica*. If you have space for one or two small trees, a good choice would be *Cercidophyllum japonicum* or perhaps the lovely yellow-leaved *Catalpa bignonioides* 'Aurea' or again the slightly larger *Robinia pseudoacacia* 'Frisia'.

Essential herbaceous plants would be *Hosta sieboldiana elegans*, one or two rodgersias, and ligularias. For the marginal beds, *Peltiphyllum peltatum, Osmunda regalis*, bog primulas and even perhaps, as it is so slow-growing, *Lysichiton camtschatcense* (the smaller white one) would all be excellent choices.

With regard to the tender exotics, it is most unlikely that there will be room in a small garden for a greenhouse or conservatory, so there is a limit to the quantity of plants that one can grow which have to be overwintered indoors. Three of the tender exotics, however, can be recommended as house plants: the datura, the banana *Musa ensete* and the aquatic plant *Thalia dealbata*. There is absolutely no reason why owners of small gardens should not grow these three, which will make splendid additions to the garden in summer and unusual companions indoors in winter. And if you get as much pleasure out of the tender exotics as I have done you will undoubtedly go on to try more varieties.

All the plants mentioned above could form the basis for a planting scheme in any garden, and the larger the garden the more one could expand upon it. I will therefore now concentrate on the main features of each layout, and mention only additional recommended plants for each of the different plans.

It is really only in gardens of about forty feet or less that there is not sufficient space for a hedge as a boundary, and so if possible you should plant one or adapt an existing one. I have suggested earlier how to deal with walls and fences if you cannot avoid keeping them.

In small gardens there are really only two places for a pond – at the end of the garden, where it is reached by a winding path and partially screened so as to be an unexpected feature, or more centrally, where it can be enjoyed from the house. If the second option is chosen then be sure to include plenty of evergreens so that the pond remains attractive in winter. In any event, the overall design should be very simple in a garden of this size.

Medium-Sized Gardens
(Around a Hundred Feet Long)

•

T his seems to be quite a common size for many town and city gardens, but the width can vary from a reasonable forty feet down to as little as twenty feet. It is necessary with these long and very narrow gardens to break them up into a series of compartments – not, as is so often done, with trellis or straight rows of conifers, but with large shrubs and clumps of bamboo and such like. I would recommend that some of the hedging plants be used for this purpose, as their main function here is as screening. Take the path from one side to the other to give an impression of greater width. It will also help considerably in such a garden to vary the levels – for instance, the central section could be lower than the adjoining ones. This would simply involve moving soil from the area you wish to lower to the adjoining areas. Remember that if you move a foot of soil in this way you will create a difference in levels of roughly one and a half feet, because you have raised the adjoining areas by six inches each.

Another way to treat these narrow plots is to have a dramatic contrast of planting such as a miniature woodland section composed mainly of trees through which the path could wind, or even a bamboo grove or jungle. To create such an area the planting must be particularly bold and should not contain too many different species.

Where you have a reasonable width of forty feet, compartmentalization is unnecessary. One of the most attractive layouts for a garden of this width is to have two ponds, one at each end of the garden, linked by a stream which is crossed in the middle by a winding path, so that the path and the water features form a figure-of-eight. This may seem to be devoting a lot of the garden to water, but there is still a surprising amount of space for planting and seating. You might have one of the pools in a very open sunny position and the other in dappled shade for contrast, with appropriate and contrasting plantings around them. The sunny pool should be positioned close to the house, from where it can be enjoyed. In one garden I made to this design I planted bamboo on both banks of the stream to one side of the bridge so that it formed a tunnel over the water, giving a very mysterious effect; whilst to the other side, which was open, I planted gunnera on one bank and osmunda on the other.

In a garden of this size you are not in any way restricted in what you can grow, and my recommendation of planting in threes should be adopted with herbaceous plants. Essential trees would be first the Indian horse-chestnut (*Aesculus indica*), *Populus lasiocarpa*, *Eucalyptus niphophila*, and possibly *Acer macrophyllum* at the end of the garden, as it is the largest of these. Among the shrubs I would include *Hydrangea aspera* or *sargentiana*, *Pieris formosa forrestii* 'Wakehurst' or *Pieris formosa* 'Forest Flame', *Mahonia japonica* or *lomarifolia*, a camellia, *Rhododendron macabeanum*, *Leycesteria formosa*, *Sambucus racemosa* 'Plumosa Aurea', either *Corylus maxima* 'Purpurea' or *Cotinus coggyria* 'Royal Purple', and *Cornus alba* 'Elegantissima'. A garden of this size should have some of the larger bamboos such as *Phyllostachys aurea* or *mitis* and perhaps for contrast the lower-growing *Sasa palmata*. With regard to the herbaceous plants which might be added to the basis which I recommended earlier of hostas, ligularias and rodgersias, I suggest you include acanthus, *Crambe cordifolia*, hemerocallis, *Inula magnifica*, lilies, rheums, *Smilacena racemosa*, and a veratrum.

Polygonum cuspidatum 'Spectabile'

Hibiscus moscheutos 'Southern Belle'

Tetrapanax papyriferus

Rheum tanguticum

Acanthus mollis latifolius

Arundo donax 'Variegata'

Canna generalis 'Wyoming' and *Melianthus major*

Embothrium coccineum

For the marginal beds I would add gunnera, *Lysichiton americanum*, petasites, *Astilbe rivularis*, some irises and the arum lily zantedeschia.

As to tender plants, the medium-sized garden should be large enough to accommodate a conservatory or greenhouse, so the range of possibilities is greatly increased. As well as the datura, the banana and the thalia, I would grow the ginger *Hedychium gardnerianum*, the tree fern *Dicksonia antarctica*, *Canna generalis* 'Wyoming', *Melianthus major* (though this could be left outside if protected), ricinus (which would be grown from seed annually) and *Arundo donax* 'Variegata'.

Large Gardens

•

V ery large gardens, perhaps up to a few acres or so, through mere size alone, entail a great deal of maintenance work, but it saddens me when I see them neglected and overgrown and think of the marvellous and exciting things that could be done with them. Even gardens of this size can be maintained much more easily with the style of gardening which I am advocating. If vast areas of lawns and huge flower beds and countless rose bushes are dispensed with, both labour and expenditure are reduced drastically. The cost of planning and planting a very large exotic garden, though undoubtedly considerable, would be more than compensated for by the wonderful effects that could be achieved.

It goes without saying that water should play an important role, and one of the loveliest of natural-looking features that would only be possible in a garden of this size is a woodland glade or dell. In the open countryside this would be a clearing in woodland, often with a stream or pond at the bottom of a dip or hollow, and the same effect should be sought in the garden. The appearance of a clearing in woodland can be created by the use of trees and tall, free-growing shrubs. When expertly done with some of the beautiful subjects such as we are dealing with in this book, the effect will even surpass that of nature. Imagine walking along a path winding its way through a leafy garden with here and there some eye-catching plant or feature, and finally turning a corner to enter a natural amphitheatre where perhaps a cascade splashes and gurgles into a pool round which are lush and leafy ferns and other moisture-loving plants enclosed by the hanging wood.

It would be pointless for me to make recommendations about the planting of such gardens when the possibilities are so great, for every plant I describe in this book is worth growing and so many of them could be grown in a garden of this size. What I have done, therefore, is to provide throughout this book a number of illustrations of plants which associate particularly well with each other. There are of course many other possibilities, but the ones shown here are among the most striking and attractive.

What to Do with Existing Plant Material

•

F or those of you who decide to venture into this form of gardening but who have or inherit a garden which is already planted, here are a few suggestions as to what to do with any existing plants.

First, trees: unless these are particularly attractive either in shape or leaf I would recommend their replacement. It is impossible to grow anything under certain trees when they are large – beech and willow are among the worst offenders. The soil under them is bone dry, the shade too heavy, and it is usually impossible to dig a hole because of the roots. Small trees can be removed easily and at little expense, but large trees may be listed or protected and it may be illegal to remove them, so check with your local council first. Trees in neighbouring gardens can be a nuisance if their branches overhang too much. I believe the law usually states that anything over six foot can be removed, but again it is better to check first. Apart from this, trees in neighbouring gardens are usually an advantage in that they form a background and may give valuable wind protection.

Any unattractive shrubs, unless they are on the boundaries where they also may provide shelter or hide existing walls or fences, should be removed. Those worth keeping should, if not suitably placed, be repositioned. If they are rather large it is advisable to prune them first to help them recover from the move. Deciduous shrubs can be transplanted any time between November and March, but evergreens should be moved in early spring, around April.

Any herbaceous plants worth keeping can be used to fill in gaps until such time as more interesting replacements can be obtained. If they need to be moved this can be done at any time of year except on hot summer days, providing they are watered first and lifted with a substantial amount of earth on the roots.

Newly planted climbers take a few years to get going and any undesirable ones should be replaced only gradually so that there are no large areas of bare wall or fence. Plant the new climber relatively close to the one you wish to get rid of. As the new plant develops, cut back and eventually remove the old one to give the replacement room to grow.

Always remember when disposing of plants that they may be welcome presents for your neighbours.

Culture – The Hardy Exotics

•

The hardy exotics are of the easiest culture and will grow happily in all but the very bleakest parts of the country, where gardening of any kind is strictly limited. Advice about the needs of individual plants as to soil characteristics and so on is given in Chapter Five; but the vast majority will grow in average garden soil provided it is neither too dry nor waterlogged. And, whatever you are growing, soil is much improved by the addition of leaf-mould or peat, which gives it a better structure and helps it retain water in dry weather.

All hardy deciduous plants will survive any winter, but some evergreens may suffer in severe conditions. It is not just the cold which is the cause of damage, but also the cutting winds. In bad winters, therefore, it pays to give a little protection to certain evergreens, such as phormiums, in the form of a mulch and straw or bracken, and, if the garden is very exposed, temporary screens. Bamboos in general dislike wind and should be placed in the most sheltered areas of the garden.

The Tender Exotics

•

N one of the tender exotics described in this book can really be said to be difficult to grow. But of course they will be killed off by frost so anyone who grows them will need to be ready to act fast on warnings of frost either at the beginning or the end of summer.

Obviously, if you live in an area which is exposed to frost and generally cold, the number of months when you can have the tender exotics in the garden is very limited, and for this reason those who live in such areas will want to concentrate on growing hardy exotics, with perhaps a few tender subjects to give that extra exotic touch in summer. But it is perfectly possible to create a truly exotic garden with hardy plants alone.

In the south and west frost does not intrude so deeply into the summer months, and so the scope for growing tender exotics is correspondingly greater. Some people are lucky enough to live in western maritime areas where frost is virtually non-existent and tender plants can be kept in the garden all year round, except in particularly bad winters. Of course the site

(Opposite) *Phormium tenax* (above) and *Hosta sieboldiana* 'Elegans' – two plants of very different outline which emphasize the architectural qualities of bold foliage

will also need to be sheltered, but a surprising number of people live in such an enviable environment, and the scope they enjoy for creating an exotic garden is almost unlimited. Remember, however, that if you are intending to grow many plants which need to be taken indoors during the winter, you should still grow a large stock of hardy exotics, especially evergreens, to avoid denuding the garden too much.

The tender exotics in general require only a reasonable soil and adequate watering to flourish. There is no particular trick to growing them, and anyone who follows the more detailed advice about the individual species given in Chapter Five should be rewarded with some handsome specimens. The easiest way to grow them is in pots or tubs which in summer can either be placed around the garden or buried in the ground, making their removal indoors in autumn very simple. Plants like the datura also make very decorative container plants for the terrace or patio. When confined to containers these plants should be grown in a good loam-based soil such as John Innes No. 3 which compensates for the root restriction. However much one enriches soil in containers it will become exhausted of nutrients after some years and should then be replaced. Gross feeders such as the datura and banana will also need to be given regular liquid feeding in spring and summer when in full growth.

Some of the tender exotics, such as the ginger (*Hedychium*), will survive the winter in the south and west, providing the roots are protected with a mulch and straw or bracken. The frost will cut them to the ground, but they will shoot again the following spring provided the roots have not been destroyed. The only drawback is that they often develop so late in the season that they will generally not flower when treated in this way, so their decorative value is partially lost. *Bergenia ciliata* is evergreen if kept frost-free, but will otherwise defoliate, though its stems are frost-hardy. By protecting such plants from frost we can enjoy them for a much longer period.

Cannas are usually lifted in late autumn and dried off, then kept in a cool, frost-free place until February, when they are potted up and started into growth at about 60°F. It is true that they require a resting period, but I find it unnecessary to dry them off. They can be kept in pots indoors and all but the newest shoots should be cut back. They will then come into growth in early spring and will have made sufficient development to be planted out some time in May, even though they have been overwintered at only 45°F. The roots of cannas do not spread a great deal and they are the easiest of plants to lift and pot up at the end of the summer.

In fact, all the tender exotics can be treated in this way rather than being permanently confined to containers. It takes slightly longer to plant out a subject in, say, May, and return it to its winter quarters of a container indoors in, say, October, but it may be preferable – particularly in certain areas of the garden where you want vegetation to be especially dominant – to avoid having a container interfering with the overall scheme. As I have suggested, containers can be buried; but planting out and repotting does not seem to disturb these plants in general, and in some cases does not even check their growth.

It may seem a great deal of trouble to move plants out into the garden and back again at the beginning and end of every summer but, compared with the constant labour inolved in maintaining a flower bed, the trouble is minute. And, considering that the number of plants involved is fairly small, the beautiful effects they add to the garden more than compensate for the effort involved in looking after them.

General Maintenance

•

One of the many merits of exotic gardening is the comparatively small amount of maintenance.

Usually one of the most time-consuming jobs in the garden is weeding. If you grow plenty of the recommended ground covering plants, such as hostas, weeds will be kept to a minimum. Some people however, like to have clearly defined clumps of plants with a narrow space around each one. This does enhance them and allows them room for expansion, but the exposed area of soil will meanwhile be prone to weeds, and so a few inches of ornamental bark will need to be applied. This is not unattractive and will eliminate most weeds.

Another very time-consuming task in most gardens is lawn mowing. Many people in their obsession with large areas of grass forget to take into account the amount of work lawns involve. It is for this reason that I would limit the lawn to as small an area as can be made do with. Remember that in summer it will require cutting twice a week in order to keep it in good fettle. If neglected, even best-quality turf will eventually become coarse. One of the best lawn treatments, especially for turf which has become off-colour or yellow, is an application of sulphate of iron and sulphate of ammonia, which will change it to a healthy dark green in a matter of days.

So far as soil condition is concerned, an annual dressing of manure or compost is best, because it has bulk and improves the structure of the soil. Chemical fertilizers will do as a temporary measure but cannot be used indefinitely. The lush growth of an exotic garden takes rather more out of the soil than the average garden and this has to be replaced. Trees and shrubs should be given a good dressing of bonemeal or hoof and horn when planted, and will need only an occasional top dressing thereafter. Do not mulch heavily around the trunks of trees or shrubs; it can damage or even kill them. Herbaceous plants, on the other hand, benefit from the substantial mulch because they are comparatively shallow-rooted (goodness in the soil leaches down through it). Another of the advantages of good mulching is that it substantially reduces frost penetration, maintaining the soil at a higher temperature and promoting earlier growth.

Exotic gardening produces a vast amount of leaf litter in winter, and this makes superb compost. The heap should be completely covered to retain as much heat as possible, and, to help the breaking down of the material, you should apply one of the special chemical compounds every foot or so. In some instances the compost will be broken down sufficiently to be used the following season, but it is usually better to leave it for a full twelve months. If you cannot accommodate a compost heap, one of the best manures is commercially available compressed cow manure. It is safe to use and completely inoffensive.

The Plants

•

Trees, providing the right ones are chosen, should need no attention other than the removal of any dead or damaged branches as necessary. Shrubs may require some annual pruning, either to improve their shape or to encourage better, stronger growth. With deciduous shrubs this is best done in winter when the framework of the plant can be seen clearly. With evergreens it is advisable to prune in early spring before growth begins.

Clumps of herbaceous plants which have become too large should be divided in winter, but this should only be necessary every three or four years, depending on the vigour of the plant. The best method is to lift the clump, insert two large garden forks back to back, and slowly prise the clump apart. Most herbaceous plants can be treated this way, but plants which take a long time to become established, such as veratrums and acanthuses, require different treatment. Do not lift the whole clump from the ground, but remove only the section you want to replant. First use a fork to loosen it and ease it away from the main section; then use a spade to sever it and lift it away, with as much soil as possible, and to carry it to its new hole. Fill in the gap left with good soil.

Bamboos take a few years to get established before making real headway. The hole in which they are to be planted should be liberally filled with manure and bonemeal or hoof and horn. If after some years they need to be divided this should be done in April. A very sharp spade is required, and the larger the portions to be removed the better, if they are to be replanted elsewhere. In some cases it is better to cut the canes right down to encourage the growth of new ones, but this should not be necessary if the ground is very moist and the site fairly sheltered.

Most climbers require no attention for a few years other than training in the desired direction. Once well established, however, some will benefit from pruning, especially the more vigorous ones, such as *Vitis coignetiae* and *Actinidia chinensis*. With these, quite severe pruning will sometimes be necessary for the sake of the plant as well as the owner.

The tender plants that are confined to containers should be potted on as soon as their roots have filled the pot. With fast growing subjects like the datura and the musa this will be quite frequently – probably twice a year. When they have become large enough for 24-inch pots or tubs, they should just be given an annual top dressing. This involves removing the top few inches (or as much as can be removed without damaging the roots) of the old soil and replacing it with rich new soil. These are really the only two plants that will eventually require containers of this size – all the other tender exotics can be divided like ordinary herbaceous plants. If after several years daturas or musas begin to deteriorate, the daturas can easily be propagated from cuttings, and the musas replaced by younger plants grown from seed.

Ponds

•

With artificial ponds, the soil of the marginal beds will need to be replaced every three or four years. This is because it becomes sour and will rot the roots of even bog-loving plants. It is probably best to carry out this work in late autumn, just as the plants are beginning to die back. Lift all the plant material and place it on plastic sheeting and then remove all the soil from the beds and leave it somewhere out of sight where it can be allowed to dry out (it can be used again at a later date with manure added). Divide any clumps of plants that have become too large, and before replanting wash as much of the old soil as possible from around the roots with a hose or by dipping in a bucket. Place a layer of soil in the bottom of the bed and then replant the bed, filling around each clump as you go. Finally, water the plants, preferably with a watering can with a rose attached.

Obviously it is desirable that the water in the pond should be as clear as possible, especially if one has fish. Bright sunlight encourages the

Blechnum chilense (above) and *Asplenium scolopendrium* – two
moisture-loving ferns for sun or dappled shade which highlight
the variation in leaf character within one family of plants

formation of algae, so a pond is best situated in dappled shade. But the best way of keeping water clear is to circulate it, as would be done for a cascade or waterfall.

Pests

•

The majority of the plants discussed in this book are rarely prone to disease due to their vigour, but one or two are sometimes troubled with pests. Rheums can be badly infested with blackfly, and if they do become so they should (as should any other infested plants) be watered with a systemic pesticide – not sprayed, which usually scorches the foliage. This type of pesticide is taken up with the sap of the plant and is a much more efficient eradicator. It can also be used to treat daturas, which are sometimes infested with whitefly or a little beetle that hides in the growing tips of the shoots and deforms them.

Slugs and snails can be a great problem, devouring entire plants, and it is far better to find and destroy their hiding and breeding places than to destroy them individually. Piles of rubbish or stones (anywhere that is dry) are the places where they are to be found, so examine such hideouts in winter when they hibernate. In summer they can be caught in the act if you go into the garden at night with a torch – they are generally found on the underside of foliage. Slugs may be easier to control with the pellets that are available and many can be destroyed if you sink lids filled with beer in the ground by the plants affected.

The brevity of these sections on maintenance should indicate just how easy it is to look after an exotic garden. It is the informality that works in the gardener's favour. Plants allowed to grow in profusion generally look after themselves and, while the formal garden looks terrible if the plants are allowed to break the constraints of the design to which they are supposed to conform, the informal garden is all the better for such exuberance.

I like to picture the exotic gardener with his or her feet up enjoying the play of the waterfall and the abundance of shapes and colours all around, while in the neighbouring gardens people struggle with recalcitrant lawnmowers and break their backs over beds and borders that somehow never quite look as they should.

CHAPTER FOUR

The Conservatory and Terraria

•

This short chapter is aimed at both the haves and the have-nots. Some people are fortunate enough to have a conservatory or are in a position to consider building one, and they have a clear advantage over those who have to make do with a greenhouse or the house itself in the cultivation and enjoyment of the tender exotics. Others will not have a garden at all, but if they dream of having one frustration can be alleviated to some extent by creating an indoor garden in a terrarium.

The Conservatory

•

If we are honest we have to admit that our long winters prevent us from venturing into our gardens for many months, during which time we can only admire them from the comfort of our homes. The climate therefore regulates when we can use our gardens, as well as what we grow in them. In the conservatory or greenhouse, however, we can create whatever climate we wish – both for ourselves and for the plants we grow.

The Victorian heyday of the conservatory or 'winter garden' is long gone, but on a more modest scale conservatories are becoming increasingly popular as an extension of the home. However, we do not yet seem to have got round to exploiting their advantages to the full. I hope that this book will help to rectify that situation by showing that with tender exotics we have a range of splendid subjects for the conservatory which do not have to be kept at a high and therefore expensive temperature.

Plants grow far better in conservatories and greenhouses than they do in the home because the levels of light and humidity are higher. In winter many houseplants become drawn and spindly. It helps to mist-spray them, but this will not totally combat the dryness of central heating. (In the home, houseplants should always be grouped together rather than scattered – this enables them to create a micro-climate around themselves, helping each other to survive.) The choice of plants for growing in conservatories must be based on the temperature range that can be maintained. Most houseplants require a minimum temperature of 55–60°F. This is a high and expensive temperature to maintain in a conservatory or greenhouse in winter as there is a great deal of heat loss. Subtropical or exotic plants require a minimum of only 45–50°F, and are therefore far cheaper to maintain. A 1° rise in temperature requirement adds many pounds to the heating bill at the end of winter at temperatures over 50°F. A collection of tender exotics can be just as attractive as one of tropical plants, and of course they have the added advantage that when grown in containers they can be moved out onto the terrace or into the garden in summer, making it more attractive and unusual. It is for this reason that I feel so strongly about advocating the cultivation of these plants, which have the merit of being both highly decorative and versatile. They earn their keep.

Choosing a Conservatory

•

Conservatories nowadays vary tremendously in style and size. At the lower end of the scale, a light weight, aluminium-framed, plastic-covered conservatory can be purchased for as little as a hundred pounds, while at the other end there are beautiful Victorian-style buildings of wood, glass and brick which cost

Fatsia japonica (above) and *Bergenia cordifolia* – two plants for a
shady spot, both evergreen and shiny-leaved. The *Fatsia* (above)
complements the *Bergenia* below it, which would be dull on its
own, though it is a good ground cover plant

thousands. The main factor when choosing a conservatory will, of course, be cost, but bear in mind that an attractive conservatory will add value to your home and is therefore an investment. Polythene lasts only a few years but is cheap to replace. It does not, however, transmit or retain heat as well as glass, and metal frames are more susceptible to temperature changes than wood. If time were available a conservatory could be built relatively easily and cheaply by anyone with average woodworking skills, but if appearance is of considerable importance then it would be better to choose one from one of the several well established conservatory and greenhouse manufacturers. Style will also obviously play a part, and the design of the conservatory should harmonize with the house.

Conservatories are far easier and more practical to heat than greenhouses, especially full-span ones, because there is a much smaller area of glass and therefore much less heat loss. Also, because a conservatory adjoins the house, it benefits from both the house's heat and shelter, but it must be in a more-or-less south-facing position.

Other than heating, the main rather obvious but surprisingly often overlooked advantage of a conservatory as against a greenhouse is that you walk straight into it from the house instead of trekking across the garden – a blessing on a freezing cold winter's day. It is extremely pleasant at such times to sit in the comfort of a conservatory surrounded with lush greenery and protected from the elements.

Heating and Shading

•

H ot-water pipes or radiators will always be the best method of heating conservatories and greenhouses, especially in terms of the health of the plants, and gas is probably the cheapest fuel. If the house has a central heating system it is an easy matter to add an extension for a conservatory, but it is vital to have an independent thermostat so that the temperature in the conservatory can be regulated. This is economical in the long run, as it avoids any unnecessary waste of heat. Bearing in mind that the minimum temperature required for the tender exotics is only 45–50°F, it will be found that except in the coldest months of the year (usually January and February) the heating will probably be on only at night.

If hot-water systems are not possible, then the best of the alternatives is probably the range of thermostatically controlled greenhouse heaters that run on propane gas. These are now widely used in commercial horticulture. This is not a cheap system to run in very cold weather, but it is still cheaper than electricity.

Whatever method of heating is adopted I would strongly recommend the use of bubble polythene sheeting for lining the conservatory. It is not very pretty, but it cuts down the heat loss considerably and can reduce heating bills by a third. Special fasteners are supplied by some manufacturers so that it can be properly fixed to either metal or wooden structures.

Shading will be necessary in the summer months, from about June to September, to prevent scorching of plants especially those close to the glass. It also reduces the temperature, which can become overbearing in the middle of summer even when ventilation is used. Roller blinds are best in that they will accommodate a change in the weather, but if costs must be kept down there are special whitewashes available (some green) which will serve the purpose quite adequately.

Layout

•

The layout of the conservatory will largely depend on its size and the amount of space that can be devoted to plants after any furniture, permanent or otherwise, has been taken into account. As well as plants in containers, which in summer can be moved onto the terrace or around the garden, in large conservatories it is desirable to have some permanent occupants, such as bougainvillaeas, abutilons and hoyas, or maybe some citrus fruit trees. These are best grown in beds either at ground level or raised, preferably with a wall of rocks. These beds are generally positioned along the sides of the conservatory, but if space permits you might also consider a central bed, perhaps of oval or round shape. When constructing these beds ensure that they have adequate drainage in the form of a foundation of broken brick or rubble – a depth of about eight inches should suffice.

Terraria

•

As a lover of growing things, I should hate to be without a garden, but plant lovers who through force of circumstances do not have one need not despair. There remains the option of indoor gardening.

Plants do not generally do so well in the home as they do in the conservatory because of the lower levels of both light and humidity, but there is one method of providing a sufficient level of both these elements, and that is in the terrarium. Terraria are simply miniature greenhouses, evolved from the Wardian case, which was used to bring back living plants from abroad when they had to survive long sea voyages. They also became fashionable objects in Victorian drawing-rooms by which time they had become rather more decorative in their design.

The close atmosphere of these structures enables anyone to grow even the most delicate and exotic of plants, but disappointingly they are seldom seen furnished with such subjects. Most of the terraria that are available nowadays are very decorative and usually very expensive hand-made items that would grace any home, but very attractive terraria can be made very cheaply using an aquarium. To my mind they make particularly good containers for an indoor garden since their simple design in no way detracts from the beauty of the internal planting. In addition, a large

A terrarium, showing:

Philodendron scandens   Syngonium wendlandii
Codyline terminalis   Alocasia x amazonica
Stromanthe amabilis   Amthurium crystalinum
Scindapsus pictus argyraeus

aquarium will house a greater range of plants and is much easier to plant up and attend to than most of the more elaborate ready-made terraria.

Buy an aquarium fitted with a metal roof designed to house the small incandescent tubes that are usually sold to brighten up the lives of tropical fish. A good-sized aquarium of three feet long, fifteen inches wide and twenty inches deep will require light and heat from five cool white 20-watt fluorescent tubes and four 10-watt incandescent bulbs. It should be lit for a maximum of eighteen hours a day. Thus the terrarium can be placed anywhere in the room, and need not be positioned so that it gets sufficient natural light. Tropical plants need high temperatures and humidity to flourish, which are extremely expensive to provide in a conservatory or greenhouse. This type of structure makes possible the cultivation and appreciation of these plants albeit on a small scale – within a reasonable budget.

Nothing could be easier to maintain. Once planted, it will need no attention other than possibly watering once a month. A list of some of the most suitable plants (in terms of both their slow growth or small size) now available appears at the end of this chapter.

Planting a Terrarium

•

A s the container is watertight, drainage material is necessary, and fine gravel is best. Put a layer about an inch and a half thick across the floor of the terrarium. The best soil to use is one of the lightweight peat-based composts generally available now, but this must then be given a generous sprinkling of pieces of charcoal to keep it sweet, and a little silver sand to ensure that it stays porous.

As the terrarium is best set against a wall, the plants in it will be viewed mainly from the front and therefore some elevation of the soil towards the back of the terrarium is desirable. This avoids having to step the plants according to height from the front, enabling you to have one or two taller ones in the foreground. A depth of about two to three inches in the front and four to five inches of soil at the back should suffice.

Before putting the plants in, loosen the outer roots and spread them a little so as to help them become established more quickly. Do not put all the soil in at once, but do so gradually as you plant the terrarium up. As you put each plant in, gently firm the soil around it. Finally, when the planting is complete, water the whole with a mist spray and replace the top.

When buying plants be sure to check with your supplier that they all like roughly the same conditions in terms of heat, light and humidity – for instance, ferns and ivies prefer a cool, shady environment, while any flowering plant needs plenty of light. Choose plants of different form and habit so that you can create plenty of contrasts within the terrarium. Avoid using too many flowering plants, as these will generally have to be replaced quite often, either because they become too invasive or because they cease to flower and look unattractive. Plants with exotic foliage are among the best subjects for terraria, but it is also fun to add unusual subjects, such as orchids and the Venus fly trap (*Dionea muscipula*).

Terrarium Plants

•

 ny of the following plants can be grown together as they like the same warm, close conditions. The following notation has been used to indicate form and habit:

U = upright
S   = spreading
Cl = climbing
Cr = creeping
F   = flowering

Aglaeonema 'Silver Queen'   (S)

A compact plant with oblong, pointed, dark-green leathery leaves with bold silvery markings.

Alocasia × *amazonica*   (U)

Deep bluish-green glossy leaves with scalloped margins and prominent silvery ivory-white ribs and margins, purple underneath.

Alocasia cuprea   (U)

Shield-shaped, glossy, quilted leaves of a metallic silvery-green with deep bluish-green vein areas, purple underneath.

Anthurium crystalinum   (S)

Heart-shaped, rich dark-green velvety leaves with silver veining.

Anthurium schertzerianum   (S and F)

Waxy, oblong, pointed leaves and bright scarlet, waxy, long-lasting shield-shaped flowers with a tail like a pig's.

Asplenium nidus   (S)

Bird's nest fern; long, broad, glossy, light-green leaves sprouting from a central crown.

Bromeliads (various)   (S and F)

Most are shaped like the top of a pineapple. The leaves may be striped, banded, or spotted, and all have different flowers. After flowering they die but produce offsets. Mostly they are epiphytic (they grow on trees in their natural environment), but some, including the smaller *Cryptanthus*, are terrestrial and consist of a flat rosette of leaves.

Calathea crocata   (S and F)

A low plant with shimmering, bronzy-green, wavy-edged leaves and bright-orange waxy flowers like those of an aphelandra.

Calathea musaica   (S)

A small plant with oval, pointed leaves of light green with a fine network of checkered bars.

Calathea ornata 'Sanderiana'   (U)

Long-stalked, oval, dark bluish-green leaves with fine pink stripes, which mature to white, purple underneath.

Calathea picturata 'Argentea'   (S)

A low plant with oval, pointed, silver leaves with a bold dark-green border.

Calathea tuxtla   (S)

A low plant with oval, pointed, dark rich-green leaves with three silver bands, one central, the others near the margin.

Caladium (various)   (U)

Thin, papery, heart-shaped leaves in various colours and markings, the most striking of which is white with green veins. They grow from tubers like a potato and need a resting period during winter, when they should be stored like a bulb.

Chaemadorea elegans   (U and S)

A lovely little slow-growing palm with bamboo-like leaves fanning towards the top of the stem.

Cocos weddelianum   (U and S)

A small palm with fine, feathery leaves; slow growing.

Cordyline terminalis   (S)

The small forms of this plant available nowadays retain the characteristic fan of dark bronzy-red leaves, the more central ones boldly and brightly banded with dark and light pink.

Ctenanthe oppenheimiana 'Tricolor'   (S)

The oblong leaves have longish stalks and are dark green with silver-grey bands and large irregular areas of white, with the wine-red undersides glowing through.

Dieffenbachia (various, small)   (S)

The so-called 'dumb cane' has large, oblong, leathery leaves, variously marked, with thick fleshy stems. After a few years they will become too large.

Dracaena godseffiana 'Florida Beauty'   (S)

Rather like a miniature laurel, but the small leathery leaves are almost covered with creamy white blotching.

Dracaena sanderiana   (U)

The elegant stems carry whorls of dark-green pointed leaves with bold white margins.

Episcia cupreata (various)   (Cr and F)

Rather like an African violet but the hairy leaves have silver markings and the flowers are bright cherry red.

Fittonia verschaffeltii   (Cr)

A ground-hugging plant with oval, matt, green leaves with a network of rose-coloured veins.

Fittonia verschaffeltii 'Argyroneura'   (Cr)

As above, but the leaves are of a shiny bright green with silver veins. A miniature form of this is available.

Hypoestes taeniata   (U)

This dainty plant has thin stems and small dark-green leaves spotted with pink.

Maranta repens   (Cr)

This small 'prayer plant' has oval, green, ground-hugging leaves with brown blotches which point upwards at night.

Orchids (various)   (U and F)

Numerous small kinds are available nowadays. The flowers are usually waxy and long-lasting, variously coloured, and often spotted or striped. They like varying temperatures and this should be checked when buying.

Rodgersia podophylla

Scindapsus pictus argyraeus   (Cr and Cl)

A slow creeper with shimmering dark-green waxy leaves, spotted and edged with silver.

Sinningia regina   (S and F)

Like an exotic gloxinia, this plant has oval, bluish-green, velvety leaves with ivory veins, and a profusion of nodding violet flowers.

Stromanthe amabilis   (U)

Oblong shiny leaves, banded bluish-green and silver-grey.

Syngonium wendlandii   (Cl)

A climber with thin, papery, three-lobed, pointed, deep-green leaves with central white veins.

Datura cornigera

Canna iridiflora 'Ehemanii'

Ricinus communis gibsonii

Phyllostachys nigra

Hydrangea aspera

Canna 'Firebird'

Phormium tenax 'Purpureum'

Cardiocrinum giganteum

CHAPTER FIVE

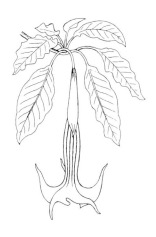

The Trees

•

y selection is rather brief, mainly because most people have space for only a limited number of trees. Also, there are relatively few trees that are of exotic appearance.

Acer negundo 'Variegatum'   (North America)   30 feet

This is probably the best of white-variegated-leaved trees. Although not as vigorous, it is much more attractive than the yellow-variegated form *A. n. elegantissima*. The serrated divided leaves are bordered with white, and in the form *A.n.* 'Flamingo' this is beautifully tinged with pink. This variety makes a beautiful shrub, but pruning is required to achieve this and a second summer pruning will improve and lengthen the coloration.

Acer macrophyllum   (Northern California)   60–80 feet.

This large- and handsome-leaved maple, known as the Oregon maple, is a large and fast growing tree. The leaves especially in younger trees are as much as a foot across – they have prominent lobes and are a smooth dark green. The flowers and seed cases are also very decorative. It is recommended only for larger gardens.

Aesculus indica   (India)   60–80 feet

The Indian horse-chestnut is one of the finest of all trees. It is far more refined in leaf than any of the other horse-chestnuts. The leaves, which are shiny and comparatively smooth-edged with reddish stems, almost resemble a schefflera. It should be grown to six feet before allowing the branches or crown to develop. There is a variety called 'Sydney Pierce', which has a darker leaf but it is somewhat difficult to obtain.

Ailanthus altissima	(China)	60–100 feet

The well known Tree of Heaven is another large and fast growing tree, but I prefer to grow it (as with *Paulownia tomentosa*) as a pollarded specimen – that is to say, each winter it is cut almost to the ground and just one shoot is allowed to develop. This will possess leaves far larger than if it is permitted to grow into an ordinary tree. It is of almost palm-like appearance with a circle of pinnate leaves three to four feet long in pollarded specimens. These leaves make a lovely contrast to the solid heart-shaped leaves of the paulownia. Ailanthus is one of the easiest of trees to grow, actually preferring a poor soil.

Catalpa bignonioides 'Aurea'	(Southern USA)	20–30 feet
Catalpa × *erubescens* 'Purpurea'	(Southern USA)	30–45 feet

The Indian bean tree, *Catalpa bignonioides*, is in my opinion a rather coarse, unattractive-leaved tree, but these two coloured-leaved forms are far nicer. The first and more commonly met with is the yellow-leaved *Catalpa bignonioides aurea*, with smooth, rounded, very shallow-lobed leaves. It is slow growing and although it will eventually make a small tree it is much more attractive when grown as a shrub, though of course pruning will be necessary to achieve this. Far less often met with is *Catalpa* × *erubescens purpurea*. Its leaves are of a much more refined, broader shape and have a dark purplish tinge when young, which fades gradually as the leaves mature. It will make a fine tree but makes an even nicer shrub with hard pruning. All catalpas like full sun and moist soil; their only slight drawback is that they are somewhat late in leafing (usually the end of May).

Cercidophyllum magnificum   (Japan)   20–30 feet

Most of you will have seen *Cercidophyllum japonicum*, but this is a much rarer tree. It is more or less identical except that the leaves are noticeably larger. These are heart-shaped and about three inches across, but it is the character which is so appealing, the graceful spreading branches bowing towards their extremities. Sun or dappled shade, and, more important, a moist soil.

Davidia involucrata   (Central and Western China)   40–65 feet

The well known pocket handkerchief tree is a stunning sight when hung with its myriad large white bracts. If you have the patience and are young enough to wait twenty years for it to flower, then it is a must. But even as a foliage tree it is attractive with its four-inch crinkled serrated leaves. It is also known as the dove or ghost tree.

Eucalyptus niphophila   (Australia)   20 feet

The 'alpine snow gum', as it is known, is probably the most beautiful of the hardy gums. The ovate leathery leaves are nice, but the tree's loveliest feature is its bark. In older trees it flakes to produce a marbling of grey, green and cream. In contrast, the young branches are a lovely dark polished red overlaid in spring with a white waxy bloom. Although hardy, like all the gums it benefits from shelter from strong winds, especially when young, and pruning at this stage of some of the lanky shoots will produce a bushier, less spindly tree.

Eucalyptus pauciflora   (Australia)   20 feet

The hardy gums are ideal subjects for the subtropical garden, their evergreen foliage making them of particular value. Most are grown for their striking and colourful bark, especially *E. niphophila. E. pauciflora*, though it does have a very attractive white trunk, also possesses handsome, large, oval leaves of the typical bluey-green colour and leathery texture. A sunny position and shelter are preferable for the first few years, and any moist but well drained soil.

| *Gymnocladus dioicus* | (East and Central USA) | 60–80 feet |

The Kentucky coffee tree, so called because its seeds have been used as a substitute for coffee, is very beautiful but – sadly – rarely seen. It bears long, airy, fine-stemmed sprays of small oval leaves, which are pink-tinged when young. This is one of the few trees that prefers partial shade, and although rather slow growing is very desirable.

| *Koelreuteria paniculata* | (Northern China) | 30–60 feet |

The golden rain tree or Pride of India can perhaps be said to look like an ailanthus with deeply serrated leaves, or possible like a rhus. However, it is more refined than both of them and, as its name implies, has lovely yellow flowers in large, upright panicles. It also has good autumn colour – altogether a tree with all the desirable qualities.

| *Meliosma veitchiorum* | (Northern China) | 30–40 feet |

This rare and beautiful tree is quite distinct in leaf from anything else. The large (2½ feet) pinnate leaves are like some exotic unprickly mahonia and once seen are never forgotten. It grows best and fastest in mild, sheltered gardens, but this should not deter any of you from having it. Sun or dappled shade and a rich moist soil are best.

Paulownia tomentosa (syn. *imperialis*)   (China)   30 feet

The 'foxtail' tree is a fast grower with beautiful soft, rounded, shallow-lobed, downy leaves that remind me very much of the tender linden tree, *Sparmannia africana*. Although beautiful as a tree, especially in flower (if the buds survive the winter), I much prefer to treat it the same as the ailanthus, that is, to prune it within a few inches of the ground in late winter or early spring, and when it breaks into growth allow only one shoot to develop. In this way it will make a shoot six or eight feet long clothed with leaves from twenty to thirty-six inches across (leaves on unpruned trees are at most ten inches across). It is best to allow the tree to grow unpruned for the first few years so that it is well established when cut back; in this way the largest leaves are obtained. Paulownias require a sheltered position in full sun and moist, rich soil.

Phoenix canariensis   (Canary Islands)   15 feet

Trachycarpus fortunei (below) and *Phoenix canariensis* are the only palms known generally to be hardy in this country although the Chilean wine palm is said to be so too. But *Phoenix canariensis* is the only other palm available commercially at present, and I have only seen comparatively small plants of it – that is to say, not yet having formed a trunk. It is, however, a most attractive 'feather' palm and makes a lovely contrast to the 'fan' palm. It is a relative of the date palm, which it very closely resembles.

Populus lasiocarpa   (China)   30–45 feet

This is by far the loveliest of all the poplars and has easily the largest leaves. These are up to a foot in length, heart-shaped, with lovely red stems and veining. This tree likes a warm sunny position and moist soil.

Robinia pseudoacacia 'Frisia'   (North America)   30–60 feet

This is the best of all the yellow-foliaged trees, staying bright late into the season. It makes a stunning golden splash grouped with the shrubs *Sambucus racemosa* 'Plumosa Aurea' and *Corylus avellana* 'Aurea'. The leaves are small and oval but are heavily produced, weighing down the branches. These are rather brittle and so this tree should be planted away from strong winds. Full sun and moist but well drained soil are advised.

Trachycarpus fortunei   (China)   10–20 feet

I have included the Chusan palm in this section for, although of slow growth, it is ultimately of tree proportions. It is perfectly hardy but should be given protection for the first few winters after planting in the form of straw or bracken placed on its crown at the base of the leaf stalks. This is the only large palm to be seen growing outside in this country and it is one of the best large subjects for the exotic garden. In the ordinary garden it looks quite out of place, but mixed with other exotic-looking things such as phormiums and the like it is superb. The leaves are like an open fan some two and a half to three feet across on long stalks – hence the name 'fan' palm. The slow rate of growth is an advantage in that this plant is much more attractive when small, with its leaves almost touching the ground. Plant evergreen shrubs behind it on the north and west to protect it from strong winds. It will flourish in moist soil. When it becomes taller underplant it with the evergreen fern *Blechnum chilense* or *Bergenia ciliata*.

Peltiphyllum peltatum (above) and *Lysichiton americanum* – two waterside plants for sun or shade with large, lush leaves of contrasting character. Both flower before the leaves have really developed

The Shrubs

•

There is space in the average garden for a reasonable number of shrubs and they are essential in forming the framework of the garden and in disguising the boundaries. They are also invaluable in helping to create mystery and creating different areas in the garden. The following shrubs have been chosen either for their large or lush foliage or for their exotic blooms. Some have colourful foliage, and a considerable number are valuable evergreens, such as the phormiums, included in this section because of their size.

Aralia elata   (South-East Asia)   9 feet

The angelica tree, or 'devil's walking stick' as it is sometimes called, has thick, straight, spiny stems with enormous compound leaves about three feet long. It makes a nice subject for the centre or the back of a bed where the shorter plants will help to hide the ultimately bare stems. Because the leaves are produced only at the tops of the stems it is far better, if space permits, to plant, say, three plants of varying heights, thereby producing a much more leafy planting which could then be a foreground subject.

Far more beautiful and, unfortunately, expensive are the two variegated forms of this plant, the so-called golden and silver aralias, whose small, pointed leaflets are bordered by yellow or white. The latter is generally considered the more beautiful.

Aralias should be grown in dappled shade in moist but well drained soil as they will not tolerate waterlogging, especially in winter. The golden form is *A. e.* 'Aureovariegate', and the silver *A. e.* 'Variegata'. White flowers are produced in long panicles which are most decorative in the unvariegated form; this form can also be cut to ground level when it becomes too tall and leggy, and it will then shoot again.

Camellias	(Japan and China)	4–6 feet and more in mild locations

Camellias started their lives in this country cosseted in glasshouses – our Victorian ancestors treated many plants this way until they realized their hardiness. They are popular shrubs, attractive for their lovely glossy evergreen leaves as well as their single or double flowers, which range from white through various shades of pink to red. These are born in late winter and early spring, usually quite prolifically. Camellias are woodland plants and so prefer shady positions and acid soil.

The range of hybrids available nowadays is enormous and as they are such familiar plants I will not discuss them further. However, I believe that the single forms which resemble the native species are the more beautiful; there is a lovely one called J. C. Williams which has blush-pink flowers.

Cercis canadensis 'Forest Pansy'	(North America)	6–8 feet

This is a fairly recently introduced plant and is a form of the American redbud. Its delicate stems carry deep reddish-purple, heart-shaped leaves about four inches long which retain their colour all season. It produces pale-rose pea flowers in May or June when a little developed, and, although rather scarce and expensive at present, it is well worth seeking out. A sunny position, preferably a little sheltered, is required.

Cornus alba 'Elegantissima'	(China and Japan)	6–9 feet

Although common, this is one of the nicest of white variegated shrubs, and I can think of no better companion to one of the purple-foliaged shrubs such as *Cotinus coggyria* 'Royal Purple' or *Corylus maxima* 'Purpurea'. The pale, grey-green, oval, pointed leaves are distinctly bordered with white. It is the easiest of plants to grow and soon makes a fine specimen. Sun or shade suits it but it grows lushest in very damp situations. The foliage takes on a pink tinge in autumn and it is well known for its red winter stems.

Corylus avellana 'Aurea'   (Europe)   6 feet

The golden form of the hazel is possibly *the* brightest golden-foliaged shrub. It should be grouped with other golden or variegated plants such as the sambucus or the lovely golden-variegated bamboo *Arundinaria viridi-striata*. For some unknown reason it is not very often available in nurseries – certainly not, I am sure, because it is unpopular. It likes a sunny position and will stay bright all through the season.

Corylus maxima 'Purpurea'   10–15 feet

The purple nut or filbert is one of the finest purple-leaved shrubs and makes a superb companion to white-variegated ones, especially *Cornus alba elegantissima*. The dark-purple leaves, similar to those of the beech, fade a little by summer so to keep the colour going it is a good idea to have *Cotinus coggyria* 'Royal Purple' (below), which comes into leaf some weeks later but retains its colour and beauty till the autumn. *Corylus maxima purpurea* carries purple nuts in autumn and catkins in winter. It likes full sun and reasonable moisture. It can be pruned severely if necessary.

Cotinus coggyria 'Royal Purple'   (Mediterranean)   8–10 feet

This is the purple form of the 'smoke bush', so called because of its fuzzy plumes of tiny flowers. The oval leaves (from two to three inches long) are in whorls and of a rich dark purple, making a striking companion for white-variegated and especially silver-foliaged plants. It seems to benefit from occasional pruning, especially of any long growths. Full sun but poor soil seem to suit it best.

There is a recent hybrid called 'Grace' with leaves twice the size but of not such rich colouring; its drawback is that its hybrid vigour has resulted in a fast-growing weighty-foliaged plant very susceptible to wind damage.

Embothrium coccineum   (South America)   10 feet

The Chilean fire bush is one of the most striking of flowering shrubs, bearing a profusion of brilliant orange-scarlet tubular flowers in May and June. It is semi-evergreen and of rather upright growth. The varieties 'Lanceolatum' and 'Norquinco Valley' are somewhat hardier than the type, which is really only hardy in the south-west of England. The plants should be grown in dappled shade and moist soil, but above all sheltered from cold winds.

Eriobotrya japonica   (Japan)   12–15 feet

The loquat is an evergreen shrub with long, shiny, wrinkled leaves with serrated margins. It is best grown against a wall or on the edge of the garden. In warm summers heads of richly scented whitish flowers are born. This shrub rarely fruits in this country but it is worthwhile just for the foliage. Although it will grow in full sun it is healthier in dappled shade.

Fatsia japonica (*Aralia japonica*)   (Japan)   4–10 feet

This is a well known but I think very underrated evergreen shrub. It thrives in shade under trees and soon makes a handsome specimen.

Often mistakenly called the 'castor oil plant' (which is in fact ricinus – see page 160) the shiny deeply lobed leaves are about a foot across, quite tropical-looking and very prominent in winter, when it also produces handsome sprays of creamy white globular flowers. When it becomes tall and much branched the leaves become smaller and it loses some of its beauty. I find it better at this stage to cut it down to about a foot when it will soon sprout into a low and much more attractive plant. There is a creamy white variegated form which, although it is said to be tender, I have found to be hardy in the south. However, it is expensive and of no great beauty in my view.

Fuchsia 'prodigy'   5 feet

I really do not care for the large-flowered hybrid fuchsias usually referred to as florists' varieties, and anyway they need to be grown more or less permanently under glass. But the more elegant though smaller-flowered hardy types are much more to my liking, and look much less out of place in the garden. Fuchsia 'prodigy' is particularly lovely in that it is tall (up to five feet) and of upright habit. The flowers have brilliant crimson sepals and purple semi-double skirts. Hardy fuchsias are cut to the ground in cold winters but regrow strongly from the base. If, however, they are grown in mild localities or overwintered under glass they will grow much taller and form trunks with flaking bark. They like a sunny position and do well against a south-facing wall. There is another smaller variety which many people like called *F. magellanica* 'Versicolor'. Its attraction lies in its foliage, which is grey-green with coppery pink tinging, especially when young. The flowers again are crimson and purple.

Hibiscus syriacus   (From Syria to the Far East)   6 feet

Most of us are familiar with the exotic forms of this flower made into garlands to welcome visitors to Hawaii, but some quite hardy, albeit less flamboyant, forms of this shrub can be grown here. There are coloured varieties in shades of lilac and pink, but to my eye the most beautiful is the form with white petals with a deep crimson basal blotch – a striking combination. The flowers are three or four inches across and are produced in late summer and last until the frosts. The only drawback with these shrubs is that they come into leaf very late in the season, usually in late May; but this should not discourage anyone from growing what is really one of the most

(Opposite) *Robinia pseudoacacia* 'Frisia' (above) and *Sambucus racemosa* 'Plumosa Aurea' – two plants for full sun, both having bright golden foliage. Such plants should be grouped together to light up an area of the garden

exotic-looking flowering shrubs. They should be given the sunniest position possible in the garden. The most sumptuous hibiscus of all, though, is *H. moscheutos,* which is tender and is therefore included in that section.

Hydrangea aspera and *Hydrangea sargentiana*   (Himalayas and China)   5–8 feet

I dislike intensely the common pink and blue *macrophylla* varieties with their coarse foliage, but here are two vastly superior and more beautiful plants. Their main beauty lies in their sumptuous velvety leaves, which in *H. sargentiana* are of rounded outline with serrated margins and in *H. aspera* are more oval, pointed and smooth-edged. *H. aspera* is the shorter and of more compact growth. *H. sargentiana* is inclined to become leggy, although it does sprout from the base and it is best to remove very long leggy shoots to encourage this. *H. aspera* is of altogether darker coloration than *H. sargentiana,* the foliage being very dark green and the lovely 'lace-cap' flowers a deeper pink. These shrubs must have shade and moisture. Although *H. sargentiana* is said to be rather tender, I have found it to be hardy in the south.

Leycesteria formosa   (Himalayas)   6 feet

The rather inappropriately named 'Himalayan honeysuckle' has an almost bamboo-like quality, with its smooth, arching shoots bearing lush, pointed leaves. Its beauty is much enhanced by large purplish bracts which almost conceal the bunches of pendant white flowers. It may be cut to the ground in bad winters but will shoot again in the spring. If this is not done its old branches should be cut out entirely to allow the new ones to ripen. Grow in sun or dappled shade in good moist soil.

Magnolia delavayi   (China – South Yunnan)   25 feet

The common types of magnolia are beautiful, their almost swan-like blooms poised on the bare branches. I particularly like the white ones. But here is a magnolia grown not for its flowers but its leaves. These are a beautiful grey-green, oblong and leathery, evergreen, from about twelve to eighteen inches long. Like some of the large-leaved rhododendrons, it is rather tender and may be damaged in severe winters even in the south. This plant will only make a shrub in all but the mildest localities, where it will grow into a large tree. Other than in these places it should be grown as a wall shrub, and the ground around it should be well mulched in winter. I find it helps with this and large-leaved rhododendrons to cover them in winter with fine plastic netting, which can give a surprising amount of protection. Dappled shade seems to suit it best.

Magnolia tripetala   (North America)   15 feet

The 'umbrella tree' is another magnolia grown for its foliage, though in this case it is deciduous. Despite the name it will for most of us be only a large shrub. However, it is quite fast growing and its whorls of long leaves are as much as twenty inches by ten in size. Like the loquat, it is a good substitute for people who like but cannot grow large-leaved rhododendrons. Sun or dappled shade.

Mahonias   (China – Yunnan)   6–10 feet

Mahonias are worthy of space in any garden. I find it difficult to choose a favourite. Most are hardy but a few are somewhat tender, though they seem quite tough once established. They have several qualities – attractive evergreen foliage, rather holly-like but less prickly and arranged in whorls; and yellow racemes of usually scented flowers, erect in some species and pendant in others. One of the commonest is *Mahonia japonica*, an easy and inexpensive plant which usually makes a very bushy specimen. *Mahonia lomarifolia*, a favourite with many, is more refined in leaf but has a much stiffer habit and is inclined to be comparatively leggy. It is said to be somewhat tender and is a much more expensive plant. Naturally, as evergreens, they are valuable in winter and they have the additional value of flowering at that time as well. They will grow in sun or shade and will take pruning if they get out of hand.

Phormium	(New Zealand)	6 feet

The New Zealand flaxes are important architectural plants for the subtropical garden. Their stiff sword-like leaves are a marvellous contrast to the many solid or round leaves of other plants. The dull-coloured flowers are produced on huge spikes which overtop the leaves by several feet. The largest and hardiest is the plain green form, of which Goliath is a vigorous clone. Here the seven-foot leaves are topped with a ten-foot flower spike. But to my mind the most beautiful is *Phormium tenax* 'Purpureum', whose foliage is a lovely dark-red purple, though the colour is very variable and good strains should be selected. Of the variegated kinds the most commonly met with is *P. t.* 'Variegatum', but the best is *Phormium tenax williamsii* 'Variegatum', which possesses much more prominent yellow variegation. Both this and *P. t.* 'Purpureum' have foliage up to about the six foot mark but there are a lot of smaller varieties in tones of pink, red, salmon, orange and bronze. All phormiums like a sunny position in moist soil away from strong winds, and in all but the mildest areas they should be protected with a good mulch.

Pieris formosa	(Western China and North-East Burma)	10 feet

What more could one want in a shrub? It has attractive, glossy, evergreen leaves, and in April and May it produces grape-like clusters of white flowers followed soon by the brilliant red new leaves, which retain their colour for some weeks, eventually turning to pink then cream then finally green. The variety *P. f. forrestii* 'Wakehurst' has slightly larger leaves but is not quite so hardy as *P. f.* 'Forest Flame'. Pieris are woodland plants liking dappled shade and lime-free soil, preferably in a west-facing position away from morning sun. This is a shrub that should be in every garden.

Pittosporum tenuifolium 'Purpureum'   (New Zealand)   5 feet

I have included this shrub for two very good reasons. First because it is a compact evergreen (the only purple-leaved evergreen other than *Phormium tenax purpureum*); second, because it is the only purple-leaved shrub I know that will grow in some shade. The small, shiny, curly-edged leaves are at first green but change to a dark purplish colour. It is said to be somewhat tender, but has recently come through some very severe winters. It provides a lovely foil for white variegated things such as the silver aralia (*A. elata variegata*).

Rhododendrons   (Himalayas)

These popular plants would need an entire book to themselves, so I have selected only those with the finest foliage. The species with the largest and most beautiful leaves of all is undoubtedly *R. sinogrande*, a magnificent plant with dark-green glossy leaves as much as three feet in length. It is unfortunately rather tender and will grow well only in mild localities. In London and other places with a warmer micro-climate it can be grown, though it will not develop the enormous leaves that it does in favoured localities such as Cornwall. If attempted by people in London or the south, it must be given a spot sheltered from north and east winds and must also be protected in winter – give it a generous mulch and lay straw around the roots, and, as mentioned for *Magnolia delavayi*, cover the entire plant with fine plastic netting supported and secured with canes.

For those not wanting such a performance, the best and largest-leaved of hardy rhododendrons is *R. macabeanum*. This has leaves about a foot long with a brownish felty underside, as opposed to silver in *R. sinogrande*; it has lovely creamy-yellow blooms which it will produce quite freely, unlike *R. sinogrande*, which flowers only when of large proportions, which it will only reach in the west. Another hardy beautiful-leaved plant is *R. fulvum*. This looks just like a smaller version of *R. sinogrande* and has lovely blush flowers with a dark blotch.

Rhododendrons are woodland plants and must have dappled shade and acid soil.

Sambucus canadensis 'Maxima'   10 feet

We are on the grand scale with this giant member of the elder family. With ordinary things it would look out of place, but with the other giants such as the gunnera and lysichitum it is superb, especially when sited near water. It is true that contrasting leaf sizes give emphasis to one another but large plants in scale with each other are very dramatic. A visitor to my garden once said that he felt as Alice must have done when she ate the piece of mushroom which the caterpillar gave her to reduce her size. This shrub should be pruned hard back in winter to achieve the best foliage effect of its huge cut leaves. Treated this way it will make several feet of growth annually and produce white flower heads a foot across. A position in full sun and moist soil are required.

Sambucus nigra 'Purpurea'   6–8 feet

The main attraction of this shrub lies in the colour of the foliage, which is a dark, almost blackish purple – an unusual colour in the garden. This seems to be retained in sunny situations but not in others (the leaves turning green). The divided leaves are shiny, and the flowers are in flat corymbs and of a pale pink fading to white, which contrasts pleasantly with the dark foliage. This is the only purplish shrub which in my opinion will associate well with any of the yellow-leaved ones, but to my mind the best comp#nion to it is the lovely white-splashed elder *Sambucus nigra pulverulenta*, which likes shade. *S. n.* 'Purpurea', however, should be grown in full sun.

Sambucus racemosa 'Plumosa Aurea'   (Europe)   6–8 feet

If I were to be restricted to one yellow-leaved shrub I should choose this, the golden cut-leaved elder. The bright yellow of the lovely feathery leaves lasts well through the season providing it is grown in full sun. Hard pruning of about two-thirds of the previous season's growth is necessary in winter for the best foliage effect and to keep this plant in good fettle. Other plants should not be grown too close to it as this can cause die-back, and it should never be allowed to become dry in the growing season. Grow it with *Corylus avellana aurea* and *Robinia pseudoacacia* 'Frisia' to really light up an area of the garden in full sun.

Viburnum davidii   (China)   2½ feet

This is one of the best evergreen low growing shrubs and forms a neat dome shape of veined, pointed, shiny leaves about five inches long. It will grow in sun or dappled shade. It has heads of whitish flowers, which are followed by black berries if both sexes of the plant are grown, but these are of no great attraction.

Viburnum rhytidophyllum   (China)   10 feet

The long (ten inches), shiny, evergreen leaves with their fine network of veins aren't to everyone's taste, but this tough and fast growing shrub soon makes a large specimen, and is ideal for boundaries or for hiding walls and fences. It does best in shade or in a north-facing position; if it is protected from the worst of the wind it will look immaculate all winter. This plant will take quite hard pruning should it get out of hand.

Ailanthus altissima (above) and *Paulownia imperialis*. When
pollarded both these trees produce large leaves which contrast
strikingly with each other

The Bamboos

•

Bamboos are among the best plants for creating an exotic effect, and form an essential part of the framework or 'bones' of the exotic garden. Like palms, they give that air of warmer climes – despite the fact many of them originate from countries where the winters are almost as harsh as our own. They are very graceful objects and once established form substantial clumps. Being evergreen they play an important role throughout the year. Like shrubs, they are useful in screening one's view of the entire garden, thereby helping to create mystery.

Although the bamboos listed below are hardy, it is best whenever possible to shelter them from their one dislike – wind. They often look shabby in winter but come the spring or summer and they regain their splendour with new leaves and canes.

There are basically two types of bamboo – those which produce their leaves and branches from the top downwards, such as the arundinarias; and those which do so from the bottom upwards, such as the phyllostachys. The second main distinction between them is that the stems of the arundinarias are permanently clothed with sheaths while those of the phyllostachys are naked (the sheaths quickly falling off) and ultimately more attractive, as they are sometimes coloured bright green, yellow and even black. The phyllostachys are not so wind-tolerant as the arundinarias and should be given shelter.

The most common of all bamboos is *Arundinaria japonica*, but I have deliberately excluded it for two reasons. First, it is in my opinion a rather coarse and comparatively unattractive bamboo, although it does possess the one quality of being very tough; second, it has flowered of late and subsequently died almost everywhere. This is a great mystery with bamboos – they do not flower for many years but when they do all individuals of a particular species do so simultaneously practically world-wide. The plant also expends so much energy in the process that it usually dies or looks so scruffy that it needs to be removed.

Some bamboos form clumps while others tend to 'run' at the root and can be invasive. With one exception, the lovely *Sasa palmata*, I have excluded the latter types.

All bamboos are gross feeders and so the ground should be well prepared with manure and bonemeal before planting. They must have moisture at all times and for that reason make ideal subjects for planting near water.

Arundinaria murieliae and *Arundinaria nitida*　　(China)　　10 feet

---

These two small-leaved bamboos are very similar in character, but *A. murieliae* has a more arching habit and is slightly shorter than *A. nitida*, whose canes are streaked purple. They are both ideal bamboos for small gardens but *A. nitida* requires some protection from strong winds.

Chusquea couleou　　(Chile)　　15–20 feet

This is a distinctive and highly prized bamboo, differing from all the others in that the leaves are produced in tufts on the very stiff, angular canes. When young it is very slow growing but in mild areas often achieves twenty feet. At present it is expensive and difficult to obtain but it is well worth seeking out.

Phyllostachys aurea,
P. viridis (mitis) P. nigra and *P. pubescens*　　(China)　　15–20 feet

---

The phyllostachys are the loveliest and the tallest bamboos that we can grow in this country. They are more attractive than the arundinarias in that their canes are bare, the sheaths falling off in development (the arundinarias retain them). They also possess much longer side branches, which causes them to stir in the slightest breeze.

Phyllostachys aurea has canes of bright green maturing to yellow. Its leaves are light green and from about two to four inches long.

Phyllostachys viridis (syn. *mitis*) has pale green canes and leaves about three inches long. It grows to fifty feet in its native country, China, but will achieve only a third of that development here.

Phyllostachys nigra is quite distinct in that its canes, which are at first speckled with black, eventually become all black and polished. This I think makes it one of the most distinctive and desirable of bamboos. Its leaves are about the same size as those of *P. mitis*.

Phyllostachys pubescens produces the thickest canes of any bamboo in this country. They are olive-green and sometimes as much as three inches in diameter and thirty feet high in favoured parts of Cornwall. The leaves are similar to those of *P. aurea*.

Pleioblastus (Arundinaria) viridistriatus   (Japan)   3 feet

This is a striking and pretty plant with leaves prominently banded with bright yellow. Its height makes it an ideal foreground subject and it is lovely grouped with other yellow-leaved plants. Trimming off the shoots to ground level is necessary at the end of winter to produce the best growth and colour of the foliage. It should be grown in full sun.

Sasa palmata   (Japan)   6–8 feet

This is the largest-leaved of all the bamboos (*S. tessellata* has slightly longer but narrower ones), and thankfully it is hardy as it is a firm favourite of mine. Although not very tall, its large almost palm-like leaves (up to about fourteen by three inches) are very graceful and make it quite distinct from the other bamboos. Although hardy, its large leaves will be lacerated in an exposed situation so it should be sheltered from strong winds. Its only drawback is that it is inclined to run at the root, but I find this no great problem as its runners are not deep and can easily be severed with a spade. This bamboo seems to prefer dappled shade, and, like all bamboos, plenty of moisture. It makes a lovely contrast to *A. murieliae* or *nitida*.

Semiarundinaria fastuosa	(Japan)	15–20 feet

This is the tallest of the arundinaria-type bamboos that we can grow here, and is vigorous and clump-forming. (*Phyllostachys vivax* is probably the tallest growing phyllostachys in this country.) *Semiarundinaria fastuosa* is of very upright habit with rather shortish side branches but quite large leaves (from six to eight inches). It is at present scarce in cultivation, but worth searching for because of its hardiness.

Herbaceous Plants

•

Acanthus mollis latifolius	(Italy)	5 feet

We know the acanthus to have been in cultivation for many hundreds of years – their leaves are carved on Corinthian capitals. They are very architectural and make marvellous foreground plants. *A. m. latifolius* has the largest and lushest leaves, which are long (about two feet), shiny and deeply lobed, arching out in large basal clumps. From these come tall spikes of purple-hooded white flowers, less freely than with *A. spinosus*, but I do not care at all for the narrow prickly leaves of this plant. Acanthus should be grown in full sun or dappled shade but they tend to flower better in the former. They are deep-rooted plants and resent being moved, so should be left undisturbed once planted. A moist, well drained soil seems to suit them best, and they will benefit greatly from a mulch, especially in the first winter.

Arundo donax   (South-East Europe)   8 feet

This giant reed is almost bamboo-like in appearance. Its canes are used in the making of various reed instruments. They are slightly arching and have opposite pairs of long glaucous grey leaves. Cut the canes down when they are two years old to encourage new ones. Although it is hardy, it benefits greatly from a generous mulch in winter. Grow it in full sun in moist but well drained soil. It dislikes heavy, wet clay. While on holiday in Ibiza I saw great drifts of it twelve feet and more high along dried up river banks. There is a very beautiful variegated form of smaller stature, but this is tender and so is included in that section (see page 149).

Blechnum chilense   (Chile)   3 feet

For me this is the handsomest of evergreen ferns. It is hardy but must be protected with a good mulch in all but western gardens. The leathery divided leaves are a coppery rose when young and mature to a rich dark green. It will spread slowly to form a colony and looks beautiful under the arching fronds of the tree fern *Dicksonia antarctica*. Grow it in an acid soil, preferably with plenty of leaf mould, in sun or dappled shade. If grown in a sheltered position the leaves will stay pristine all through the winter, if it is not a severe one.

Cautleya spicata (usually called *C. robusta*)   (Himalayas)   2 feet

A member of the ginger family, this is a striking plant with its yellow flowers with maroon bracts. The foliage is typically ginger-like – opposed spear-shaped blades of rich green on stiff stems. Grow it in rich soil and mulch it in winter.

Crinum moorei and *Crinum powellii*   (Natal)   3–4 feet

These are relatives of the amaryllis, which they resemble in general character except that they are somewhat larger. They have long, floppy, strap-like leaves and large trumpet flowers on thick stalks. *C. moorei* has the best foliage, with pale pink flowers, but it is not as tough as *C. powellii* and should be grown only in the south of England. There is a white form, *C. m. album*.

    Crinum powellii has rose-pink flowers but its varieties are superior. These are *C. p. album*, a pure white; *C. p.* 'Haarlemense', a light pink; and *C. p.* 'Krelagei', a deep pink. All crinums flower for several weeks and are sweetly fragrant. Their very large bulbs should be planted with their necks just above ground level in full sun, if possible by a wall, and they should be well mulched in winter.

Crambe cordifolia   (Caucasus)   6 feet

Above a large rosette of rather cabbagy but nonetheless attractive leaves rises a huge flower stem six feet high by as much across, an explosion of tiny white flowers. It likes a moist, well drained soil in full sun and looks well with other large things, especially rheums.

Eremurus robustus   (Turkestan)   8 feet

This foxtail lily is the tallest and most beautiful of the species. Its flowers are pale pink on tall slender spikes above long strap-like leaves, which are rather withered by flowering time. There are other species of smaller stature in yellow and white and numerous hybrids. Eremuruses require well drained soil in full sun. They possess very large, fleshy, spreading roots which are rather brittle and should be planted carefully just beneath the soil. They make very bold background plants, and in this position the gap they leave afterwards is not so apparent.

Filipendula rubra 'Albicans'   (Eastern USA)   6 feet

The so-called 'queen of the prairie' is usually met with in the form *F. r. venusta*, whose flowers are of a vibrant deep carmine – a colour which I find far too strong and impossible to blend with other colours, rather like some of the astilbes. But the plant here is a lovely white or very pale pink, its astilbe-like blooms a foot across held over tall clumps of lovely palmate, serrated foliage. It is almost like a giant astilbe and like those plants is magnificent by the pond side or in the bog garden. Grow it in sun or dappled shade in very moist soil.

Fritillaria imperialis 'Lutea'   (Western Himalayas)   3 feet

The well-known 'crown imperial' to my eye looks quite out of place in the ordinary garden because of its exotic appearance, but it is an ideal subject for the informal garden. Its great value lies in the fact that it flowers so early – April. The red form is the one usually seen, but I prefer the beautiful clear yellow of this one. A thick stalk rises from an eighteen-inch-high clump of leaves and is topped by a cluster of large, pendant bells crowned with a tuft of leaves rather like the top of a pineapple. Plant the bulbs in a sunny position in good but well drained soil about eight inches deep.

Hemerocallis (the day lilies)   (Japan)   3–4 feet

These very underrated lily-like plants are now becoming appreciated more – and deservedly so. They are of the easiest culture and, although each individual bloom lasts only a day, they produce a succession of blooms over a long period. The yellow-flowered varieties are mostly scented. They have been in culture for many hundreds of years in the Far East. The flowers are a culinary delicacy. Many varieties have been introduced; some of the latest (as with the hostas) are of American origin. Hemerocallis are among the best of flowering plants for the subtropical garden.

I have included two of the best species, and selected some of the best hybrids for their colour and beauty of flower shape. They will grow in sun or dappled shade in almost any soil except chalk, as long as it is reasonably moist.

Hemerocallis flava	(South-East Europe)	2 feet

The flowers are clear yellow and of a beautiful shape, with recurved petals. Its greatest quality is its exquisite scent.

Hemerocallis maculata	(Japan)	4 feet

This is a strong grower with flowers of a pale coppery hue with a dark centre.

Hybrids		3–5 feet

H. 'Stafford' is probably the best red – a lovely mahogany red with a deep yellow throat. *H.* 'Missenden' is another of more upright habit. *H.* 'Marion Vaughan' is a lovely vigorous plant with lemon-yellow flowers. *H.* 'Whichford' is an old variety with exquisite scent. It has delicate primrose flowers with elegant pointed petals. *H.* 'Dream Waltz' has flowers of peachy apricot; while *H.* 'Spanish Gold' has flowers of brilliant orange.

Heracleum mantegazzianum	(Caucasus)	10 feet

There will be some who will be astonished at my inclusion of this stately but infamous plant. But as we are considering subjects for an informal or 'wild' type of garden as opposed to an ordinary one I consider it appropriate. Looking like a giant cow parsley, its huge divided leaves form a mound in the first year. In the second year the enormous candelabra flower spike appears, with flower heads in huge white corymbs. It is said to be biennial but is often perennial, and is quite safe to grow providing the flower heads are removed before they set seed. If not you will have a 'day of the triffids'. One other caution – do not handle the plant roughly in strong sunshine: the sap is an irritant to sensitive skins and can cause rashes and an unpleasant purple staining. Grow it in dappled shade in moist ground. Its size always makes it a subject of curiosity and comment.

Hosta sieboldiana 'Elegans'   (Japan)   2½ feet

Hostas need no introduction – their popularity testifies to that. Despite the ever-increasing number of varieties available today, I still find this variety one of the best. It is probably the largest, if not the most distinctive in leaf. Its only imperfection lies in the flowers, which are not held well above the foliage. Despite this, the strongly ribbed, round, blue-grey leaves (about a foot in length) make it a must for every garden. Its coloration makes it a beautiful companion to *Ligularia dentata* 'Desdemona', and for contrast of form ferns are unbeatable. For collectors there is a stunning gold-leaved hosta called 'Sum and Substance', which retains its bright golden colour in a sunny situation. *Hosta ventricosa* 'Variegata' is the most striking of variegated hostas, possessing dark-green leaves with a white margin. *Hosta* 'Tallboy' has by far the tallest flowers of any; they attain four feet and are of rich lilac colour, held above luxuriant rich green leaves. Hostas grow lushest in very moist soil in dappled shade.

Incarvillea delavayi   (Western China)   2 feet

Lovely divided foliage and deep rosy-pink trumpet flowers are the characteristics of this exotic and individual-looking plant. It likes a well drained soil in full sun and, although hardy, should be mulched in winter. There is a similar species, *I. maiei*, but this is only half the height.

Rodgersia tabularis

Dicksonia antarctica

The author's garden, London

The author's garden, London

Phyllostachys pubescens

Inula magnifica   (Caucasus)   8 feet

This is a stately plant indeed, with enormous paddle-shaped leaves three feet long and strong stems terminating in branched sprays of yellow, narrow-rayed daisies five inches across. It is magnificent with other large things such as rheums and polygonums. It likes a sunny position in any good soil. A marvellous waterside or bog garden plant!

Ligularia dentata 'Desdemona'   (China)   3 feet

The ligularias are very decorative plants for the border, waterside or bog garden. They prefer dappled shade but their one essential requirement is moisture. *L.d.* 'Desdemona' is probably the most popular because of the colour of the foliage. When the leaves are young they are a gorgeous dark winy-purple and mature to a rich dark-green, sometimes tinged with reddish-purple on the top, while the undersides and the stems of the leaves are dark mahogany red. They are kidney-shaped, about a foot across. The flowers are orange daisies on branched stems. There is a similar variety called 'Othello' but the colouring of the foliage is not quite so nice. Lovely with *Hosta sieboldiana* 'Elegans'.

Ligularia macrophylla   (The Far East)   5 feet

This is quite distinct both in leaf and flower from all the other ligularias and is a choice and desirable plant rare in cultivation. The glaucous grey-green leaves are paddle-shaped and about two feet long, with a prominent ivory mid-rib. The flowers are yellow and are borne in a dense spike.

Ligularia × palmatiloba   5 feet

This is a hybrid between *L. dentata* and *L. japonica*, and is an improvement on both. It has deeply cut leaves of rounded outline with deeply incised margins, which are quite markedly veined, and tall clusters of orange flowers. A certain amount of shade is essential, as is plenty of moisture to prevent the foliage from flagging.

| *Ligularia wilsoniana* | (China) | 6–8 feet |

Although very similar to *L. veitchiana*, which is easier to obtain, this species does have distinctions. The rounded but slightly triangular leaves, which are deeply veined, are somewhat larger and smoother and of a darker green than *L. veitchiana*. The narrow yellow flower spikes are also taller. The leaves are about a foot across on angular hollow stems.

The lilies

Plants of stately elegance possessing an airy quality, the lilies are deservedly popular. One could easily devote an entire book to them, but as they are familiar I have selected just a few species and hybrids which I consider among the best. I have deliberately excluded the king of the race, the magnificent *Cardiocrinum giganteum* – first, because it is both expensive and difficult to acquire; and, second, because the bulbs take seven years to flower, after which they die, though they do produce offsets. It is also a plant that seems to require ideal conditions to thrive.

The lily species prefer damp and even boggy conditions, while the hybrids require a well drained soil. The soil for both hybrids and species should be rich in humus. Never plant the bulbs in winter when the soil is cold and wet, but in late autumn or early spring in dappled shade. Slugs are the big enemy and sand should be poured liberally in the planting hole. It is also advisable to move the bulbs to a new spot every two years.

Lilium canadense (Eastern North America) 4–6 feet

A firm favourite with me, this lily has the most elegant pendant blooms, of a deep yellow with maroon spots in the centre. It is a plant of graceful poise and is most attractive when planted on the margins of streams, which is its native habitat.

Lilium pardalinum (Western North America) 8 feet

The leopard or 'turkscap' lilies are grand plants of easy culture. As their name implies, they have recurved petals. The upright stems carry for half of their length many downward-facing flowers, which are of a reddish-maroon with heavily spotted orange centres. This plant is one of the parents of the 'Bellingham' hybrids, a fine race of plants. These and the 'Aurelian' hybrids, of equal quality, give the gardener a wide choice, providing something for every taste. The best form of *L. pardalinum* is *giganteum*.

Nomocharis pardanthina (Western China) 3 feet

This relative of the lilies is possibly of even greater beauty. The orchid-like blooms, which are slightly frilled, are a lovely pale pink with a spotted centre. They hang gracefully on upright, wiry stems and are from three to four inches across. This plant flowers in early summer but must have cool conditions to do well. For this reason it does better in the northern half of the country. Plant the bulbs four inches deep in lime-free soil, preferably with lots of leaf-mould, with good drainage.

The paeonias

This well-known family of plants, with its vast numbers of hybrids, is too big for me to discuss in detail, but as they possess such exotic blooms together with lush attractive foliage it would be amiss of me to exclude them altogether. I would first like to make the distinction between the two main types of paeonia, namely the herbaceous and the shrubby, or 'tree', paeonias. The flowers, which may be single or double, vary in colour through white to yellow-pink and deep crimson and are anything from six to ten inches across. The herbaceous ones grow up to about three feet and the tree paeonias up to five feet. My personal preference has always been for the single varieties, especially the white ones. Most of the herbaceous paeonias available today are the garden hybrids or 'Chinese' paeonias, and for me the most beautiful of these are the so called 'Imperial' varieties. These differ from the others in that the usual yellow stamens have developed into narrow petals, either yellow or the same colour as the petals. These are all single varieties and many have the added bonus of possessing reddish-purple-tinted spring foliage. Paeonias flower in late spring or early summer and like a sunny position in rich, well drained soil – preferably not a spot which gets morning sun, as this can damage the developing buds.

Phytollaca americana and *Phytollaca clavigera*   (Florida and China)   4 feet

The poke weeds are lush, leafy plants with very fleshy succulent stems and leaves. When established, they make large and impressive specimens, their stems topped with flower spikes – white in *P. americana* and pink in *P. clavigera*. The latter is probably the handsomest of the two, its stems turning a bright crimson in autumn. Both of them have shiny black berries in autumn. Grow them in full sun or light shade in any moist soil in the middle or back of a bed.

Polygonum cuspidatum 'Spectabile'   (Japan)   8 feet

This is one of the most strikingly beautiful plants. Its tall stems, which later branch, are clothed with leaves about six inches long, irregularly marbled yellow-cream and green. At first the bamboo-like stems rise vertically, then as their side branches develop they arch over with the weight. It must be grown in shade to prevent scorching of the leaves, and although not as invasive as the green form it does rather run at the root.

Polygonum sachalinense	(Sakhalin Island)	12 feet

This is basically a larger, unvariegated, version of *P. cuspidatum* although its leaves – about eight or nine inches long – are of a more refined shape. Like some bamboos, it is a super plant for the margins of water, but is extremely invasive. An ideal location for it would be on a small island in the middle of a large pond, where it would be restricted. It has the added attraction of small white racemes along the stems, which in the male plant are vertical. Grow it in sun or dappled shade in moist soil.

Rheum tanguticum	(China)	6–8 feet

Bold architectural plants both in leaf and flower, *Rheum* species are similar in that they almost all have large rhubarb-like leaves with serrated edges. Many have reddish-purple spring foliage and the same colour on the undersides of the leaves. The lovely thing about *R. tanguticum*, however, is that the upper sides of its leaves are also often tinged with purple, especially early in the season. The flowers, which are tall, fluffy spikes, may be white, pink or red. A similar species, *R. atrosanguineum*, has more deeply incised leaves of dark bluish-green and more imposing flower spikes in cerise crimson. These are big plants, with leaves about three feet long, but there is a lovely small species called *Rheum alexandrae*, which has small, dark-green, shiny leaves six inches long. The beauty of this species lies in its three-foot flower spike, which has large, creamy bracts which conceal the flowers. These bracts become tinged with red in late summer.

If space permits it is better to plant rheums in threes. This way a much leafier result is obtained, and, more important, a less obvious gap is left later on in the season, providing the crowns are fairly close together – say, two feet apart. Plant them in dappled shade in rich moist soil. They look good under or in front of trees, and the lovely glaucous blue-grey-leaved hostas, such as *H. sieboldiana* 'Elegans' and *H. tokudama*, make beautiful companions to the purply-tinged *R. tanguticum*.

The rodgersias

All the rodgersias are highly ornamental plants both in the border and by the waterside. They all have rather astilbe-like flowers, but, above all, variable and very decorative foliage. They all like a leafy moist soil and dappled shade.

Rodgersia pinnata superba   (China)   3 feet

The horse-chestnut-like leaves are a super bronze colour in spring and later turn green. The flowers, though bright pink, are somehow inoffensive. A lovely companion to blue-leaved hostas.

Rodgersia podophylla   (Japan)   3 feet

The star-shaped leaves of this plant are not only bronze in spring but they take on purplish tints in summer if grown in a sunny position. The fluffy ivory flower spikes are rather sparsely produced, but the shape and colour of the leaves of this plant make a lovely contrast to *R. tabularis*.

Rodgersia tabularis   (China)   3 feet

If ever a plant were to be treated with reverence it is this. Although not rare, it is not met with half so often as the other species and is comparatively slower growing, taking a few years to mature. When well established and grown in rich moist soil, its beautiful circular pale-green leaves can be as much as three feet across. It must be grown in dappled shade or the leaves will scorch and wither. The tall, ivory flower spikes are small and dense.

Mulch generously in winter and do not disturb once established. A lovely neighbour for *R. podophylla*.

Smilacena racemosa (North America) 2½ feet

Looking like an exotic Solomon's seal, this lovely plant attains its full beauty when it has built itself up into a large clump. The leafy arching stems terminate in fluffy, ivory-white, lusciously scented flowers. This plant must have shade and a lime-free soil.

Trachystemon orientale (Asia Minor and the Caucasus) 2½ feet

There are not many plants that will grow in dry shade, but this is one and the best I have met with so far. Its rough, hosta-shaped leaves, a foot and sometimes more in length, spread quickly by strong underground stems, making it the ideal ground cover plant. In windy situations its bristly leaves are inclined to bruise one another but in reasonable shelter they will stay pristine until the frosts.

Trilliums (Western USA and Eastern North America) 15–24 inches

---

These are among the most beautiful of ground cover plants. They are at their best in spring, which is when they flower. In time they will form small colonies in cool, moist woodland conditions. The most striking species is *T. chloropetalum*, which has dark green leaves beautifully marbled with pale brown. In the centre of the three leaves are erect, stalkless, crimson-maroon flowers. This plant can grow up to two feet, making it the largest of the trilliums. *T. grandiflorum*, the wake robin, is a more familiar plant and, although its leaves are plain green, the broad, pure white flowers more than compensate and make a striking companion to the maroon of *T. chloropetalum*. There is a form, 'Roseum', with rose-pink flowers and a rare double white form, 'Flore Pleno'.

The veratrums	(Europe, Siberia and North America)	6 feet

These often treasured plants, with their striking oval pleated leaves, take several years to mature, and once established should never be disturbed. It is difficult to choose between them as they all have distinct and attractive flowers. But they are all worth growing for their leaves alone, which are finest in *V. viridi*. They should be grown in rich soil in shade to prevent scorching of the leaves.

Veratrum album has large, dense, greeny-white flower heads. Those of *V. nigrum* are much the same, only narrower and a striking maroon, making it the most distinct. *V. viride* has narrow spikes of green flowers, and the whole plant is of the same uniform colour. Veratrums are nice companions to the lilies – to which family they belong – ferns, and the hostas.

Zantedeschia aethiopica 'Crowborough'	(South Africa)	3 feet

The familiar arum lily is a lovely plant on the edge of, or even in, the water. In the latter situation the roots will need to be planted at least six inches below the water, deep in the mud. This 'Crowborough' form is hardier than the type, but I would still advise mulching it well in winter if it is planted in the border or waterside, especially when first planted. The type is a lovely conservatory plant and in those conditions will also flower in winter. For the curious there is a super green, white-throated-flowered arum called 'Green Goddess', which has rather larger leaves. This must also be mulched well when planted in the border. Arums confined to pots in the conservatory will flower better if liquid-fed; in the border they should be planted in rich, moist soil. The arum lily associates well with many other waterside plants by the pond or on the margins of streams.

Waterside and Bog Plants

•

Astilbe rivularis	(Nepal and Western China)	6 feet

The astilbes are familiar moisture-loving plants, usually seen in what I find rather garish shades of pink and red. But *A. rivularis* is quite distinct from these smaller forms and is a grand plant in both foliage and flower. The six-foot arching plumes of greenish-white flowers rise above the mound of deeply divided handsome dark-green leaves with contrasting red stems. A magnificent plant for the waterside. A similar plant of smaller stature is *Aruncus sylvester*. They require dappled shade and, above all, plenty of moisture. These plants associate particularly well with the solid-leaved waterside plants such as lysichitons and even gunneras.

Gunnera manicata	(Southern Brazil)	6–10 feet

This majestic giant needs no introduction; there is nothing to equal it as a subject for the waterside. It looks stunning at the foot of a huge waterfall at Chatsworth. Understandably it would look out of place in an ordinary garden, but in the exotic garden – in scale with other large subjects such as lysichitums, petasites, and the shrub *Sambucus canadensis* 'Maxima' – it is superb. Its huge fleshy roots must be able to reach down to the water, and it is a gross feeder, benefiting from generous mulching. It grows somewhat taller in shade, though the leaves will not be any larger. The crowns must be protected in winter and this is best done by covering them with its own dead leaves, and also straw or bracken in severe winters.

Irises

The most beautiful and exotic-flowered members of this race are rather tender and are therefore included in that section. But the more ordinary kinds, though not particularly sumptuous in flower, provide foliage which is an essential contrast to the many solid leaf shapes of the subtropical garden, and especially the waterside plants. The following are among the best in flower. These irises do best in good soil and moist situations, unlike the tender ones, which abhor poor drainage.

Iris 'Monspur'   4 feet

This is a splendid plant, a vigorous hybrid with soft Spode-blue flowers.

Iris 'Ochraurea'   4 feet

This is similar in character to *I.* 'Monspur' but has abundant soft-yellow flowers. It is lovely with *Lysichitum americanum*, and one of the best and easiest to grow.

Iris orientalis   (Asia Minor)   4 feet

The foliage is lush and stiff and the pure white flowers carry a yellow mark on the recurving petals. It is probably the best hardy iris for foliage.

Iris fulva   (United States)   2 feet

This species is one of the latest-flowering irises (July) and bears beautiful brick-red flowers over its arching foliage.

Lysichiton americanum	(Western North America)	3–4 feet
Lysichiton camtschatcense	(Kamtchatka)	3–6 feet

These plants with their huge paddle-shaped leaves are a must for any garden with water. Apart from the lush foliage, the large spathes which appear in May are a striking feature. In *L. americanum* the leaves are about three feet in length and glossy, and the pointed spathes a foot high are bright yellow. *L. camtschatcense* is altogether of smaller proportions. The leaves are glaucous and the flowers have pure white spathes with green spadices. More beautiful than either of these is a hybrid between the two, as yet unnamed. It is even larger than *L. americanum*, with lovely pale-green glaucous leaves as much as six feet in length; but its crowning glory are the flowers – the spathes are a lovely cream and eighteen inches high. Unfortunately this treasure is not yet available commercially.

Lysichitums take several years to become established and reach full size and should not be disturbed once planted. The thick, fleshy roots delve deeply and they require rich boggy soil. Plant them in dappled shade on the edge of a pond or stream.

Osmunda regalis	(Great Britain)	6 feet

The 'Royal' fern, notwithstanding its beautiful appearance, is native to Britain, and is one of the most imposing of all ferns. In spring the emerging fronds are like bishops' croziers of a coppery hue, and rise vertically. As they develop they fan out, and in autumn turn a lovely gold. They are finely divided into short, narrow segments. There is a purple form, *O. r. purpurea*, which is striking in the spring, but the coloration matures to green, leaving only the stems darker. The crowns, which are a mat of roots, should be planted at the water's edge, ensuring meanwhile that they are above water level. Acid soil is required, in sun or shade.

Peltiphyllum peltatum	(California)	3 feet

In April or May the tall bristly flower stalks rise from the fleshy creeping rhizomes with starry pink flowers – a strange sight. Then as they begin to fade the leaves emerge – round, from twelve to eighteen inches across, with scalloped margins – centrally supported on long stalks like umbrellas, whence its name, the 'umbrella plant'. The roots spread to form a colony and will cover a bank right down into the water. It is one of the most decorative of waterside plants and is a good substitute where a gunnera cannot be accommodated. This plant prefers peaty soil, in sun or shade. In some situations the foliage takes on lovely autumn tints of reds and purples.

Petasites gigantea	(Japan)	3 feet

Admittedly rampageous, this is a marvellous plant for covering large difficult areas such as a dark, damp, heavy clay bank. The huge kidney-shaped leaves, up to three feet across, are lovely at the water's edge. In winter the flowers, which are frilled rosettes, sit on the ground. This plant must have heavy, wet soil and, above all, shade to prevent the vast leaves from collapsing. Not recommended for small gardens.

Bog primulas

No garden with water would be complete without a few drifts of these lovely plants. They are sound perennials and will often self-sow in the moist peaty ground they love, in sun or dappled shade. They are the perfect foil for the larger pond or streamside subjects. The following are just two of the best of a wide range available both in size and colour.

Primula florindae   (Tibet)   3 feet

This vigorous plant flowers for several weeks in summer when many of the others have finished. The tall stems carry fragrant citron-yellow bell flowers over clumps of lush, rounded leaves. It will grow even taller, up to four feet, in rich boggy soil.

Primula pulverulenta 'Bartley strain'   Western China   2–3 feet

---

This is one of the best of the 'candelabra' primulas. It flowers in early summer in whorls of great elegance of the loveliest pale salmon-pink hue.

Zantedeschia aethiopica   (South Africa)   3 feet

This arum lily is described under 'Herbaceous Plants' on page 138.

The Climbers

•

I nvaluable for covering fences, walls or unsightly buildings and other objects such as dead tree trunks, the climbers are a natural part of any garden. The following are the most striking and unusual either in leaf or in flower, and are particularly suited to the exotic garden.

Actinidia chinensis　　(China)

The chinese gooseberry is a vigorous climber with round leaves six inches across and stems with reddish bristles. It holds on by strong corkscrew-like tendrils and can climb to a considerable height. In smaller gardens it will need to be pruned quite severely after a few years but it does not object to this and in some cases benefits from it. It is ideal clambering into dead trees that would be costly to remove. To produce the fruits (Kiwi fruits) plants of both sexes are required and these are generally available. A sunny position in any reasonable soil will do. Cut out old stems where they can be replaced by younger growth.

Actinidia kolomitka　　(China and Japan)

Oval, pointed leaves about four inches long splashed with pink and white make this one of the most striking of all climbers. It must have full sun or the coloration will be sparse. Its elegant twining stems are best trained on a wall or fence.

Akebia quinata　　(China, Korea and Japan)

This evergreen or semi-evergreen shrubby climber has very attractive and distinct foliage. The leaves generally have five but sometimes seven oval lobes, three to five inches long, shiny on the upper surface and pale underneath. The small, three-petalled flowers, which are a deep red-maroon, bloom in April and are followed by unusual, chocolate-coloured seed-pods. In warm climates this plant produces fruits somewhat resembling those of the Chinese gooseberry. It grows best in mild areas, but can be grown anywhere in the south, though it will be cut back in bad winters. It prefers sun or dappled shade, and moist soil.

Ampelopsis megalophylla   (Western China)

Very rarely seen and quite distinctive in leaf, this subject somewhat resembles a larger and more robust form of wistaria. The large compound leaves reach two feet in length and are dark green. Slow to establish but rewarding. Sun or dappled shade.

Aristolochia durior (syn. *macrophylla*)   (North America)

The 'Dutchman's pipe' – so called because of the shape of the little flowers which are usually hidden by the big (from six to eight inches long) heart-shaped leaves – is almost reminiscent of a philodendron, the well-known race of house plants. Its wiry stems need support and it looks particularly nice growing on large old trees. Sun or dappled shade.

Campsis × *tagliabuana* 'Madame Galen'

This is probably the most exotic-looking flowering climber that we can grow outside in this country. The deep orange-red trumpet-shaped blooms, which are four inches long and three inches across, are borne in clusters towards the ends of the stems in late summer and autumn. It is a fast growing self-clinging climber, the foliage somewhat resembling that of the jasmine, only larger. It must be pruned hard annually to ensure good flowering. This is a cross between *C. grandiflora* and *C. radicans*, both of which have smaller flowers.

Clematis

These are very popular plants, but it is a shame that so many people choose to grow only the familiar purple and pink large-flowered hybrids, particularly in view of the fact that there is such a wide range to choose from nowadays. As they are so familiar I have chosen just a few of the more unusual examples. Clematis should be allowed to ramble over shrubs and up trees – where they look far more natural and beautiful than on trellis panels, which their foliage is not really substantial enough to cover. Their roots need to be in the cool of shade, and the rest of the plant up in the sunshine. I have included the flowering season for each variety.

Clematis florida 'Sieboldii'	(Japan)	(summer and autumn)

This is certainly the most exotic-flowered clematis, somewhat resembling a passion flower. The broad, white-pointed, well defined petals are markedly contrasted by large violet-purple petal-like stamens. One note of caution, however: it is not as vigorous as most other clematis and is best grown on a wall-trained shrub in a south- or west-facing position. And until it is established some protection of the roots, such as straw or bracken, is necessary.

Clematis macropetala 'Snowbird'	(spring and early summer)

Small, white, exquisitely shaped pendant flowers make this one of the most beautiful of all clematis. At present, unfortunately, it is somewhat difficult to obtain. I believe 'White Swan' is similar. Part of the beauty of *C. m.* 'Snowbird' lies in the fact that the slender-pointed-petalled flowers are held out on long, fine stalks.

Clematis niobe	(midsummer)

I have chosen this large-flowered clematis purely for its colour, which is a lovely deep velvety red. The petals are offset by golden-yellow anthers.

Clematis orientalis 'Jack Drake' and 'Bill Mackenzie'   (summer and autumn)

Most of you will have met *C. orientalis* with its yellow lantern flowers and silver whispery seed heads. The flowers of 'Jack Drake' and 'Bill Mackenzie' are similar and of the same shape, but much larger.

Clematis 'Wadas Primrose'   (late spring and summer)

This has creamy-white flowers with elegant pointed petals – an altogether more refined shape than, say, the more familiar white *C.* 'Marie Boisselot'.

Humulus lupulus aureus   (Temperate Europe)

The 'golden hop' is the only yellow-leaved climber we have, and is a must for 'lighting up' an area with other golden-leaved plants such as the shrub *Sambucus racemosa* 'Plumosa Aurea' and the tree *Robinia pseudoacacia* 'Frisia'. Like them, it must be grown in full sun. It is best grown on a framework or over dull and uninteresting shrubs.

Parthenocissus henryana   (China)

This pretty little climber has five-lobed, velvety, bluish-green leaves with pink-tinged silver veining. It is a delicate plant and will need help initially to start climbing. Eventually it will attach itself by little suckers and by twining. It must have shade and usually turns bright red in autumn.

Schizophragma integrifolia   (Central China)   (July)

This is related to the better known climbing hydrangea, *Hydrangea petiolaris*, but is a much rarer and more exotic-looking plant. The flowers, a foot across, consist of corymbs surrounded by large white bracts an inch and a half long – a striking feature. *S. hydrangeoides* is similar but has altogether smaller and less conspicuous flowers, with creamy bracts. Grow it in a shady spot over an old tree trunk or similar object.

Vitis coignetiae   (Japan)

This plant is well known for its brilliant autumn colour but should not be grown for that alone. The large, handsome, typical vine-shaped leaves will soon cover walls or any unsightly buildings once the plant is established. It will benefit from an occasional hard pruning, especially if the largest leaves are required; these may be a foot in length. Grow in full sun.

The Tender Exotics

•

These are the most spectacular and luxuriant subjects that we can grow in the open air in the summer months in this country. They vary in size from the lowly *Bergenia ciliata* or *Begonia evensiana*, only a foot in height, to the majestic banana *Musa ensete*, which can attain some fifteen to twenty feet. A beautiful and exotic-looking garden can be created solely by the use of hardy exotics, but it will not have quite the luxuriance of one graced with the tender subjects. When I wander through my garden here, where the sun's rays are broken by the fans of the palm tree, and the bamboos rustle in the breeze which carries the scent of the datura, I sometimes half expect suddenly to hear the cry of macaws or see an exotic butterfly glide across the path, such is the atmosphere of the scene.

A visit to the temperate glasshouse at Kew will provide an idea of the kind of garden I am describing, but the effect of those 'caged' individuals is not so atmospheric as when they have the freedom of the open air. It is surely worth trying a few of these lovely plants, which can add so much beauty, especially to a garden already furnished with hardy exotics. You will then begin to appreciate how much more the exotic garden has to offer than the ordinary formal one, which is so artificial and unnatural by comparison.

Arundo donax 'Variegata'   (Mediterranean)   6 feet

This reed is one of the most striking and beautiful of variegated plants. The canes are striped and the leaves boldly margined with creamy white. Even overwintered under glass, the lower portions of the canes become rather tatty and it is far better to cut them right down each winter (unless the plant is permanently grown in the conservatory). It will then shoot early in the year and will have made from four to six feet of growth by May, when it can be planted outside. It should be grown in full sun and looks lovely with purple phormiums or purple shrubs such as *Cotinus coggyria* 'Royal purple'. There is a splendid clump of it in the Ventnor Botanic Garden, Isle of Wight.

Bergenia ciliata   (Nepal, Kashmir and Pakistan)   1 foot

I have included this plant in this section for although its stems are hardy its foliage is frost-tender. This is far more beautiful and refined than the evergreen leathery-leaved kinds that are so familiar. The soft hairy leaves are round, a foot in length; the flowers are pale pink. One of the loveliest of low growing things, it deserves a prominent position at the front of a bed in shade or dappled shade. It looks gorgeous under the spreading fronds of the tree fern *Dicksonia antarctica* or the palm *Trachycarpus fortunei*.

Begonia evensiana (China and Japan)	1 foot

This is far lovelier than any of the bedding begonias and is almost hardy, withstanding a degree or two of frost. The olive-green, deeply veined, shiny leaves are purplish underneath, and the sprays of long-stalked iridescent flowers are a delicate blush. Grow in sun or dappled shade. It increases by little bulbils and flourishes in very mild areas.

Beschorneria yuccoides (Mexico)	8 feet

Despite its name, this yucca-like plant does in fact belong to the amaryllis family. From the tuft of grey-green leaves rises a spectacular arching flower stem, coral red with pink bracts and green bells – looks to me far more like some enormous bromeliad. It must be grown in a sunny, well drained position, such as against a south-facing wall, or set in paving where it can get well baked and set its six-foot flower stems to best effect.

Canna	4–8 feet

The cannas are widely used by city parks departments in formal bedding schemes, where they are planted in ugly masses or in rows. This spoils what are individually beautiful plants. Nothing suits them more than the informal setting of the exotic garden, where their lush banana-like foliage and exotic flowers harmonize so well with the other subjects. They should be grown in full sun in moist, rich soil.

Canna 'Firebird'   7 feet

The bright red flowers stand out at a great distance and blend well with the fresh, bright green leaves.

Canna generalis 'Wyoming'   6 feet

The most sumptuously coloured-leaved canna, this has broad, rich dark-purple leaves with a faint central feathering of green. The large flowers are a rich apricot-orange and a little strong for my liking, but the foliage is a stunning companion to the glaucous grey serrated leaves of *Melianthus major*.

Canna iridiflora 'Ehemanii'   (Peru)   8 feet

This rare plant is arguably the most beautiful of the cannas. With the exception of the flowers it is of altogether larger proportions, having the most superb leaves (up to three foot long and a foot across). The leaves contrast with the comparatively small flowers, which are a beautiful rose colour on drooping spikes. The purple castor oil plant *Ricinus c. gibsonii* (see under annuals, page 159) makes a particularly lovely companion to this variety of canna.

Canna lutea   (South and Central America)   3 feet

The main beauty of this plant lies in its flowers, which are of the loveliest clear yellow and of refined shape.

Cordyline indivisa   (New Zealand)   6–10 feet

This is the most beautiful in leaf of all the cordylines that can be grown out of doors, though it can remain there only in mild and sheltered areas. The huge rosette of leaves has long blades up to five feet in length by about eight inches wide with a prominent orange mid-rib and fine orange and white parallel lines. The stems are stiff, upright and unbranched, but this does not spoil the character of the plant because the crown is so large. This plant should be grown in a semi-shady position in moist but well drained soil. The flowers, which are white and produced in a dense long spike, are of no great beauty but the foliage more than compensates for this. There is another, rather smaller, species called *C. banksii* but this is not so beautiful in leaf.

Datura cornigera   6–8 feet

This is the most sumptuous of all flowering shrubs for the exotic garden. Its huge, white, fragrant, pendulous flowers never fail to draw attention, swaying in the gentlest breeze. The trumpets are from eight to ten inches long, semi-double, with recurved points to the petals. The large downy leaves are about a foot long on non-flowering stems, but smaller on flowering ones. It is usually grown as a shrub, but it is far more beautiful when grown as a standard. Grow a single stem, pinching out any side shoots till it has reached five or six feet, then allow the crown to develop into several side branches. These will produce far more flowers than a shrub-grown specimen, although the latter will be leafier. A succession of blooms can be had from April through to October, with only short non-flowering periods – if any.

Daturas are fast growing, greedy plants; they require a rich soil and will benefit from additional liquid feeding, especially in summer. Never allow them to become dry; stand container-grown plants in saucers of gravel and water. Daturas should be grown in full sun and if possible in a reasonably sheltered position. The name *D. brugmansia* or *knightii* is probably synonymous with *D. cornigera*. This plant is sometimes called *D. suaveolens*, which in fact has larger but single flowers without recurved petals. It should be noted that all parts of the datura are poisonous.

Dicksonia antarctica (Australia) 10 feet

This lovely tree fern can be seen thriving and even seeding itself in many sheltered Cornish gardens. It is one of the most beautiful occupants of the subtropical garden, and if space permits deserves a little glade all of of its own where it can spread its magnificent fronds, which grow up to six feet long. It looks particularly lovely with an underplanting of the super evergreen fern *Blechnum chilense*. This majestic plant should be grown in dappled shade in very moist, leafy soil.

Eucomis pole-evensii (Transvaal) 5 feet

A rare plant with six-inch-broad, long, wavy-edged leaves, above which rise stout stalks carrying extraordinary dense spikes of greenish flowers crowned with a tuft of leaves like a pineapple top ten inches across. Plant the bulb five inches deep in a warm south-facing position such as by a sunny wall.

There is a similar but smaller plant called *E. pallidiflora* which is two and a half feet high and an even smaller one called *E. bicolor* only eighteen inches high. Both of these are more easily obtainable.

Hedychium gardnerianum (North India) 5–6 feet

The gingers are grand plants, both in leaf and in flower. This, the largest that we can grow, flourishes outside in the summer months and has stout stems carrying on opposite sides fleshy leaves four inches broad and fifteen inches long. In late summer the leafy clumps are topped with ten-inch spikes of deliciously scented yellow flowers with long orange stamens. A clump of this looks magnificent in front of a large banana *Musa ensete*. There is a small but lovely species with deep bluey-green leaves called *H. greenei*. This is about half the height of *gardnerianum*. These plants must be grown in full sun in rich, loamy, moist soil.

| *Hedychium coccineum* 'Tara' | (India, Burma) | 5 feet |

This is only second in beauty to *H. gardnerianum*. It differs in that it is of slightly smaller stature, with narrower leaves and flowers with orange petals and red stamens. Its greatest qualities, however, are that it is hardier, and appears to flower earlier and more bountifully.

| *Hibiscus moscheutos* | (Eastern USA) | 4 feet |

The 'swamp rose mallow' is rarely seen but is certainly a show stopper. The huge, satiny, almost hollyhock-like flowers are six inches across and can be crimson-pink or white. They blend well with the lush, round-pointed leaves. Grow in full sun in a warm, sheltered position. This plant will do well against the house.

| *Iris consfusa* | (Western China) | 3–5 feet |

The flowers of this lovely plant are more like a cattleya orchid than an iris, with sprays of lilac-white-frilled petals with purple and orange markings. These are held above a great fan of rich green evergreen foliage. This and the following species require warm, very sharply drained positions. The best method is to build a raised bed, which will give good drainage and catch and reserve heat, baking the plants – which is what they love. *Iris wattii* has similar but larger flowers, but is even more tender.

| *Lobelia tupa* | (Chile) | 5 feet |

This unusual plant bears no resemblance to the familiar types of bedding lobelia. The tapering spikes have lovely brick-red tubular flowers with grey projecting tufts. The light-green leaves are long, pointed and pubescent. It likes a sunny position in good moist soil.

Musa ensete   (Central and East Africa)   up to 18 feet

This, the Abyssinian banana, is the crowning glory of the exotic garden, and is the largest in leaf and most magnificent of plants that we can grow in the open air in this country. It grows on the lower slopes of the mountains in its native habitat and is built to withstand much more wind than the other kinds of banana, which, when in the open, are usually seen with their leaves lacerated by the winds. *Musa ensete* is altogether a much stockier plant, with a short stout trunk and thick fleshy leaves with a prominent red mid-rib. After several years it will attain leaves of some twelve to fourteen feet in length and two and a half feet in width, and reach an overall height of about eighteen feet. I have found it to be one of the fastest growing plants I have tried. As it does not produce offsets it has to be grown from seed; once these have germinated, three-foot plants are obtained in six months. In eighteen months the largest of these will have grown to eight or nine feet high and possess leaves five feet long and twenty inches wide. For most of us the problems of both moving and housing such a large plant would deter us from growing it, but this problem need not arise if plants which have outgrown their homes are replaced with younger ones – which only costs the price of a packet of seeds.

This plant overwinters best in the conservatory but will also tolerate the environment of the home provided it is given plenty of light. It absorbs a vast amount of water to compensate for the evaporation from the huge leaves and is a gross feeder like all bananas. A rich soil is therefore required and copious watering during the period of full growth in the summer months. *Musa ensete* should be grown in full sun in a position sheltered from strong winds.

There is a so-called 'hardy' banana, *Musa basjoo*, which grows outside permanently in a few very warm sheltered gardens, but it does not possess the beauty and the wind-resistant quality of *M. ensete*. Its hardiness is to be commended, however, for I have known it even when cut to the ground by frost to shoot forth again the following season. It requires to be well wrapped up in winter with straw, and the ground around it well mulched to protect it from the frost, but it should be grown only in the south and west.

These are the only species of banana that will make proper growth in the open with us; all the other species require the constant warmth and humidity of a greenhouse.

Melianthus major   (South Africa)   3–8 feet

The distinctive character and beauty of this plant have always made it desirable to lovers of foliage. The deeply lobed and serrated leaves are of the glaucous grey-green of *Hosta sieboldiana*. In warm sheltered gardens it survives the winter but becomes leggy and lanky. It is far better to cut it down in winter; the following spring it will sprout from the base and form a bushy and much more attractive specimen. If it is left out for the winter the roots must be well protected with a mulch and straw or bracken. When allowed to grow tall it will produce maroon flowers but these are not beautiful enough to sacrifice the plant's main beauty, its foliage. *Melianthus* should be grown in full sun, and by far the loveliest companion for it is the purple canna, *Canna generalis* 'Wyoming'.

Myosotidium hortensia   (Chatham Islands)   18 inches

The Chatham Island forget-me-not is a much-prized evergreen foliage plant. The round, deeply veined, shiny leaves are reminiscent of *Hosta sieboldiana elegans*, and the flowers are forget-me-not blue. It is not an easy plant, but if fed on a liquid seaweed fertilizer it will do much better. Grow it in a sunny spot with purple ajuga and silver lamium. It may be left out in the south and west providing it is well covered with straw and bracken.

Pseudopanax (Nothopanax) laetus   (New Zealand)   5 feet

This beautiful evergreen shrub looks rather like a small bushy schefflera. The five-lobed, smooth leathery leaves, about a foot across, have purplish-red stems. Though quite a tough and vigorous shrub once established, at present it is unfortunately rare in cultivation. It likes a sunny position in good moist soil.

| *Tetrapanax papyriferus* | (Formosa and China) | 6 feet |

The 'rice paper' plant belongs to the aralia family, and the similarity to *Fatsia japonica* can be seen in the shape of the leaves. But there the similarity ends, for here we have a foliage plant of considerably greater beauty. The leaves are much larger – up to two feet across – and less deeply lobed than those of the fatsia, and when young are completely covered in a white powdery bloom. This gradually disappears from the upper surface of the leaves but remains on the rest of the plant. When it eventually becomes tall and leggy it can be cut to within six inches of the ground and will then sprout vigorously from the base and the soil. It should be grown in dapled shade in good moist soil, and looks particularly nice planted near purple cannas.

| *Thalia dealbata* | (South Carolina, Florida and Texas) | 6 feet |

I think the best way of describing this beautiful plant would be to say that it is like a strelitzia, only of more delicate build – though I refer only to the foliage. The long-stemmed boat-shaped leaves are glaucous bluey-green, and small purplish flowers overtop them by two feet. It should be grown like a reed, in soil which is a few inches below the water's surface. Although this plant will survive the winter in the south if the roots are protected, it is far better to treat it as a house plant in winter, and it makes a very decorative one. Grow it in a pot or basket, which can be submerged at the edge of the pond in the summer months and in winter can be stood in a bucket of water. It likes a sunny position in rich, loamy soil.

Tibouchina urvilliana   (Southern Brazil)   8 feet

A stunning evergreen shrub with fresh green ovate leaves covered with fine white pubescent hairs, the stems four-angled. The flowers, which are like large, rich purple violets, are produced over a long period in the summer. One of the most exotic-looking of shrubs, it does not like an exposed position.

Wigandia urens   (Mexico)   8–10 feet

This noble foliage plant has enormous oval leaves from two to three feet long. The whole plant is covered with glistening and – unfortunately – stinging hairs, and one should therefore avoid brushing against it. In the young state it is rather like a tobacco plant, but it soon develops into a woody-stemmed shrub. The mauve flowers are produced in huge racemes, twelve to eighteen inches tall and somewhat resembling lilac, but they are seldom seen in this country. It requires full sun and moist but well drained soil.

Orchids

•

lthough at present the two orchids described below are almost impossible to obtain, they are listed because situations are constantly changing and often improve.

Calanthe tricarinata   (Nepal)   2 feet

This graceful plant bears sprays of greenish-yellow flowers with prominent maroonish lips held above a tuft of bold oval leaves. It requires dappled shade and well drained leafy soil.

Cypripedium reginae (syn. *C. spectabile*)   (USA)   1 foot

This is a lady's slipper orchid with white-winged petals and a big-bellied rich pink pouch three inches across. The leaves are large, oval and pleated. It requires the same culture as the previous plant.

Annuals

•

The following are very decorative and easy to grow, and can be germinated either in a small propagator or a thermos flask of warm water. If the latter, as soon as they have begun to sprout they should be potted singly and put on a sunny window sill until all danger of frost is past, when they can be planted outside. The best time to start the seeds is February, so that the plants reach a decent size by planting time.

Hibiscus   2–5 feet

I have already described *Hibiscus moscheutos*, which is a reliable perennial, given protection, but some large-flowered hybrids are best treated as annuals. The blooms can be as much as nine inches across – especially in my favourite, 'Disco Bell', which has white flowers with central crimson blotches. It also comes in deep rose, rose, and pure white. These all attain about two feet. 'Dixie Belle' comes in similar shades. These plants like a sunny position in moist but well drained soil and reasonable shelter.

Nicotiana	(South America)	*4–6 feet*

The tobacco plants are worthy both for their beauty and their fragrance. There are several small, coloured varieties now available, but as a companion to the other members of the exotic garden *Nicotiana sylvestris* is the best. It has a large number of pendant white fragrant blooms, which are held well above the large paddle-shaped leaves. All tobaccos like a very sunny position and moisture.

Ricinus	(Tropical Africa)	6–8 feet

These are the real 'castor oil plants'. They make striking objects with other large-leaved things, especially the banana, giving a really tropical effect. The loveliest is *Ricinus communis gibsonii*, which has winy-purple star-shaped leaves from twelve to eighteen inches across. *R. c. impale* has leaves of the same size, but green with red veins and stalks. *R. c. zanzibariensis* is plain green and has much larger leaves, two feet across. These plants start off with a simple stem but later branch and become quite shrubby. They like full sun in moist soil.

APPENDICES

With the exception of *Trachystemon orientale* (which does nevertheless require shade), all large, leafy subjects require moisture, so there is no category below of plants for dry situations. Where good drainage is required this is stated in the plant notes. Only plants referred to in this book are listed here.

Plants That Need Full Sun

SHRUBS

Corylus avellana 'Aurea'
Corylus maxima 'Purpurea'
Cotinus coggyria 'Royal Purple'
Hibiscus moscheutos
Leycesteria formosa

Magnolia tripetala
Phormiums (all)
Sambucus canadenis 'Maxima'
Sambucus n. 'Purpurea'
Sambucus racemosa 'Plumosa Aurea'

BAMBOOS

Pleioblastus viridistriatus (all bamboos will grow in full sun but the rest are probably better in part shade).

HERBACEOUS PLANTS

Acanthus (all)

Arundo donax

Crinum (all)

Crambe cordifolia

Cautleya spicata

Eremurus (all)

Fritillaria

Incarvillea

Inula magnifica

Phytollaca

CLIMBERS

Actinidia chinensis and *Actinidia kolomitka*

Humulus lupulus aureus

Vitis coignetiae

WATERSIDE AND BOG PLANTS

Gunnera manicata

Osmunda regalis

Peltiphyllum peltatum

All the tender subjects with the exception of *Bergenia ciliata*, the tree fern *Dicksonia antarctica* and the rice paper plant *Tetrapanax papyriferus* prefer full sun.

Plants That Prefer Shade

•

Dappled shade, as afforded by most trees, is preferable, but many plants will grow in the shade of north-facing gardens.

SHRUBS

Camellias (all)

Cornus alba elegantissima

Eriobotrya japonica

Fatsia japonica

Hydrangea aspera and
   Hydrangea sargentiana

Mahonia (all)

Pieris

Rhododendron (all large-leaved)

Viburnum rhytidophyllum

HERBACEOUS PLANTS

Heracleum

Hosta (all)

Ligularia (all)

Polygonum cuspidatum spectabile

Rheum tanguticum

Rodgersia (all)

Smilacena racemosa

Trachystemon orientale

Trillium (all)

Veratrum (all)

CLIMBERS

Parthenocissus henryana

Schizophragma integrifolia

WATERSIDE AND BOG PLANTS

Astilbe rivularis

Lysichitum

Osmunda

Peltiphyllum peltatum

Petasites gigantea (full shade)

Stockists of the Tender Exotics

●

Most of the hardy subjects described in this book should be obtainable without difficulty (apart from some of the rarer bamboos, which can be supplied by Drysdale Nurseries), so only stockists of the tender plants are listed here.

Arundo donax 'Variegata'	Beth Chatto, Hilliers
Bergenia ciliata	Beth Chatto
Beschorneria yuccoides	The Knoll Gardens
Canna iridiflora	Burncoose & South Down Nurseries
Cordyline indivisa	Burncoose & South Down Nurseries
Datura cornigera	Long Man Gardens, Newington Nurseries
Dicksonia antarctica	Burncoose & South Down Nurseries
Eucomis bicolor	Avon Bulbs, Thompson & Morgan
Hedychium	Long Man Gardens, Newington Nurseries
Hibiscus moscheutos	Thompson & Morgan
Lobelia tupa	Fortesque Garden Trust
Melianthus major	Burncoose & South Down Nurseries
Musa basjoo	Burncoose & South Down Nurseries
Muse ensete	Thompson & Morgan
Myosotidium hortensia	Spinners
Ricinus c. gibsonii	Thompson & Morgan
Thalia dealbata	Stapeley Water Gardens
Tibouchina urvilliana	Hilliers

ADDRESSES

Architectural Plants, Cooke's Farm, Nuthurst, Horsham, West Sussex
RH13 6LH

Avon Bulbs, Bradford-on-Avon, Wiltshire

Beth Chatto, White Barn House, Elmsread Market, Colchester CO7 7DB

Burncoose & South Down Nurseries, Gwenapp, Redruth, Cornwall
TR16 6BJ

Drysdale Nurseries, 96 Drysdale Avenue, Chingford, London E4 7PE

Fortesque Garden Trust, The Garden House, Buckland Monochorum,
Yelverton, Devon PL20 7LQ

Hilliers Nurseries (Winchester) Ltd, Ampfield House, Ampfield, Romsey,
Hants S051 9PA

The Knoll Gardens, Stapehill Road, Stapehill, Wimborne, Dorset
BH21 7ND

Long Man Gardens, Lewes Road, Wilmington, Polegate, E. Sussex
BN26 3RS

Newington Nurseries, Newington, Oxford

Spinners, Boldre, Lymington, Hants

Stapeley Water Gardens, Stapeley, Nantwich, Cheshire

Thompson & Morgan, London Road, Ipswich IP2 0BA

INDEX

maintenance, 73–4

manure, 74

maples, 12

Maranta arundinacea, 31

 M. repens, 96

Masson, Francis, 20

medium-sized gardens, 65–7

Melianthus major, 44, *66*, 67, 156

Meliosma veitchiorum, 104

mowing, 74

mulch, 74

Musa, 7

 M. basjoo, 155

 M. ensete, 20, 30, *34*, 44, 64, 155

Myosotidium hortensia, 156

Nandina domestica, 20

Nesfield and Barry, 21

New Zealand flax, 6, 64, 116

Nicotiana, 25, 160

 N. sylvestris, 160

Nomocharis pardanthina, 133

Norfolk Island tree fern, 29, 30

Nothopanax laetus, 156

orchids, 96, 158

Osmunda regalis, 64, 141

ostrich ferns, 27

overwintering tender exotics, 70–3

oxygenating plants, 58

Paeonia, 133–4

palm houses, 22

Parthenocissus henryana, 147

paths, 52–3

Paulownia imperialis, 105, *120*

 P. tomentosa, 105

paving stones, 53

peaceful qualities, 4

Peltandra, 12

Peltiphyllum peltatum, 64, *107*, 142

Perilla, 25

Petasites, 67

 P. gigantea, 142

pets, 78–9

Phoenix canariensis, 105

Phormium, 40, 41, 116

 P. tenax, 6, 64, 71

  P.t. 'Purpureum', *114*, 116

  P.t. 'Variegatum', 116

  P.t. williamsii

   'Variegatum', 116

Phyllostachys aurea, 66, 122

 P. mitis, 66, 122–3

 P. nigra, *99*, 122–3

 P. pubescens, 122–3, *147*

 P. viridis, 122–3

Phytollaca americana, 134

 P. clavigera, *49*, 134

Pieris formosa, 116

 P.f. 'Forest Flame', 45, 66

 P.f. 'Wakehurst', 45, 66

Pinus excelsa, 12

pitcher plants, 27

Pittosporum tenuifolium 'Purpureum',
 117

plant collectors, 19–25

Pleioblastus viridistriatus, 123

Polygonum cuspidatum 'Spectabile', *50*,
 134